The Official Behind-the-Scenes Guide to the Hit Movie!

Dr. Seuss'

THE CAT IN THE HAT™

Written by
James Greenberg

TRIUMPH
ENTERTAINMENT
Division of Triumph Books
601 South LaSalle Street
Chicago, Illinois 60605

ACKNOWLEDGMENTS

Doing justice to this material required lots of help and patience from many. Thanks to Bo Welch and Alex McDowell for graciously taking time out of their incredibly busy schedules to talk about the film. To Cindy Chang for her guidance and tireless pursuit of just the right image and Andy Lipschultz for passing the buck and sharing his great expertise.

Also to Dawn Ahrens, Bob Baker, Ben Arnon, Richard Bloom, Kevin Campbell, Andrea Carter, Herb Cheyette, Gigi Duenas, Eddie Egan, Bette Einbinder, Elizabeth Gelfand, Beth Goss, Chante Hardesty, Helen Jorda, Bill Kispert, Randy Nellis, David O'Connor, Jennifer Sandberg, Angie Sharma, and Kim Von Hagen.

And, of course, to the crafty Cat himself, who was indeed inspiring, and the awesome imagination of Dr. Seuss, without whom there would be no movie.

Book Editorial Staff

Publisher
Bob Baker
Bailey Park Consulting

Writer
James Greenberg

Art Direction
Michael Stassus
Rockett Media

TRIUMPH ENTERTAINMENT
Division of Triumph Books
601 South LaSalle Street
Chicago, Illinois 60605

MIKE MYERS in

Dr. Seuss'

THE CAT IN THE HAT

CATS WITH HATS ONLY!

UNIVERSAL PICTURES / DREAMWORKS PICTURES / IMAGINE ENTERTAINMENT PRESENT A BRIAN GRAZER PRODUCTION MIKE MYERS "DR.SEUSS' THE CAT IN THE HAT" ALEC BALDWIN KELLY PRESTON DAKOTA FANNING SPENCER BRESLIN MUSIC BY DAVID NEWMAN SONGS WRITTEN BY MARC SHAIMAN SCOTT WITTMAN ASSOCIATE PRODUCER ALDRIC LA'AULI PORTER COSTUME DESIGNER RITA RYACK SPECIAL MAKEUP EFFECTS CREATED BY STEVE JOHNSON FILM EDITOR DON ZIMMERMAN ACE PRODUCTION DESIGNED BY ALEX McDOWELL DIRECTOR OF PHOTOGRAPHY EMMANUEL LUBEZKI ASC EXECUTIVE PRODUCERS ERIC McLEOD GREGG TAYLOR KAREN KEHELA SHERWOOD MAUREEN PEYROT BASED ON THE BOOK BY DR. SEUSS SCREENPLAY BY ALEC BERG & DAVID MANDEL & JEFF SCHAFFER PRODUCED BY BRIAN GRAZER DIRECTED BY BO WELCH A UNIVERSAL PICTURE

DREAMWORKS PICTURES   IMAGINE   PG PARENTAL GUIDANCE SUGGESTED   SOUNDTRACK ON DECCA / UMG SOUNDTRACKS   UNIVERSAL

www.thecatinthehat.com

Dr. Seuss' The Cat in the Hat movie Furniture designed by Domestic Furniture • Roy McMakin • Seattle / LA

Photography
Photography by Melinda Sue Gordon, except as follows:
Michael Garland: Page 66 (top right), 67, 69; Matt Ullman / Edge FX: Page 20, 21 (all but bottom), 22, 23, 80 (bottom); 81 (bottom) and 106; Rhythm & Hues: Page 62, 116, 117, 118, 120, 126; Universal Studios Consumer Products Group: Page 124, 125

3 1558 00276 4926

'Cat' Contents

A Cat is Born

Thanks to the Baby Boom, there were more kids running around the playgrounds of America in the mid-fifties than ever before. A lot of people felt these kids had a big problem: they couldn't read very well.

A 1955 bestseller by Rudolph Flesch, "Why Johnny Can't Read," sounded a national alarm, and a cover story in *Life* magazine by John Hersey blamed it on the "unnaturally clean boys and girls" in the bland readers used in schools all over the country.

Sally (Dakota Fanning) and Conrad (Spencer Breslin) recreate one of the most recognizable images from *The Cat in the Hat*, the iconic opening illustration of a brother and sister looking forlornly out their window at the rainy day.

Something had to be done about *See Spot Run*. Kids were no longer interested in seeing Spot run anywhere.

And that's how *The Cat in the Hat* was born. An editor friend at Houghton Mifflin Publishers challenged Theodor Geisel (Dr. Seuss to you) to write a book kids might actually want to read themselves. The idea was to create a book using a vocabulary of 225 words. Geisel said he'd take the list of words home with him to La Jolla, California, and play around with it.

Geisel was under contract to Random House but his crafty publisher, the legendary Bennett Cerf, agreed to loan him out, and eventually wound up acquiring the rights to the book.

Meanwhile, Geisel was shocked to discover that there were no adjectives on the list of words. This was going to be harder than he thought. He told his biographers, Judith and Neil Morgan (*Dr. Seuss & Mr. Geisel*, Da Capo Press), that he read the list forty times and got more and more discouraged.

He decided he would pick out the first two words that rhymed and they would be the title of his book. The words just happened to be "cat" and "hat." And the rest, as they say, is history.

It took Geisel a year of "getting mad as blazes and throwing [the manuscript] across the room," but finally *The Cat in the Hat* was published in March, 1957 to widespread acclaim. *Newsweek* called Geisel "the muppets' Milton," and Hersey called the book a "harum-scarum masterpiece" in *Holiday* magazine.

In a house like any other
Something magical would happen
To a sister and a brother

Screenplay of *Dr. Seuss's The Cat and the Hat*

7

ABOVE
Sally and Conrad might look like angels but she's a control freak and he's just plain out of control. At heart they're good kids who really need someone like the Cat.

The response at bookstores was equally ecstatic. The first 100 copies at $1.95 a piece flew out of Bullock's department store in L.A. like hot cakes and 250 more were rushed in. (These were big numbers at the time.) Sales averaged about 12,000 a month and kept building.

After three years, the *Cat* had sold almost a million copies, and was translated into French, Swedish, Chinese and Braille. Geisel brought the Cat back by popular demand in 1958 with *The Cat in the Hat Comes Back*, but that proved less successful than the original.

The amazing thing about Geisel's masterpiece is its staying power. Generation after generation delight in the lovable anarchy of the Cat. Parents who grew up on it (those Boomers again) read it to their children and now their grandchildren.

By 2000, it had sold 7.2 million hardcover copies in the United States alone, making it the ninth best-selling children's hardcover book of all time. It has now been translated into nineteen languages.

The Cat in the Hat was so successful that it spawned a division of Random House called Beginners Books. By 1960, the company had published 18 titles, with sales exceeding one million dollars a year, and helped revolutionize the children's book business and the way kids read.

"That's how it all began, to give kids pleasure reading," says Theodor Geisel's widow, Audrey S. Geisel. "The underlying idea was to make them love reading and go forth on their own."

"Ted worked on it and worked on it and had quite a hard time, but he did it and it took off like a rocket."

AUDREY S. GEISEL, widow of *The Cat in the Hat* author Theodor Geisel

Chasing Their Tails

After scoring a big hit with *Dr. Seuss'*
How the Grinch Stole Christmas in 2000,
Academy Award® winning producer Brian Grazer
thought he might have an easier time convincing
Theodor Geisel's widow, Audrey S. Geisel, to let him
make *The Cat in the Hat*. "Well, it was a little
easier," jokes Grazer, "but only because *The Grinch*
was so hard.

For *The Grinch*, Grazer and his partner in Imagine Entertainment, Ron Howard, had trekked down to Mrs. Geisel's home in La Jolla, California, to make their pitch. "We did a ton of begging," recalls Grazer.

While Grazer was filming *Dr. Seuss' How The Grinch Stole Christmas*, he became determined to do *The Cat in the Hat,* but the rights were owned by DreamWorks, the company co-owned by Steven Spielberg, Jeffrey Katzenberg and David Geffen.

The Geisel estate suggested talking to Spielberg. "He said, 'Why don't we try doing it together?'" says Grazer.

So it was back to Mrs. Geisel. "I still had to do a lot of begging. The only difference was this time instead of me going down to La Jolla, she flew up and talked to us."

Grazer convinced her that he had a strong vision for the project and eventually won her over. Later, during shooting, Mrs. Geisel actually came to the set and spent a few hours in the art department looking at the curious contraptions her husband's book had inspired.

"It was very gratifying because she really responded to it all," says production designer Alex McDowell. "She said she wanted her house to look like this. I'm not sure if she was kidding or not."

CONCEPT ART

"The challenges were enormous," sighs Grazer. "First of all, you're paying homage to Dr. Seuss, so you can't mess anything up.'

Grazer wanted the Cat to be the ultimate guy to be around, someone who could take the kids -- and the audience -- for this huge roller coaster ride. "I thought about it for quite a while, then I brought the guys in who wrote *Grinch*, and they helped conceptualize. But it took about ten drafts before we could actually get to a starting point."

The thing that was really daunting was taking a story built around a vocabulary of 225 words for first-graders and turning that into a feature-length film. Subplots had to be created, which the book didn't address.

"People who haven't read it lately have this fond memory of an elaborate story that doesn't exist,' says one of the screenwriters, Alec Berg.

From the beginning, Grazer understood that the action had to be bigger with more at stake. "Just from producing 60 movies, I knew it had to have some scope." says Grazer, "Particularly because this is a comedy adventure movie."

The writers invented a dog as a plot device to get the Cat and the Kids outside the house and into the real world. When the dog runs away with the lock to the Things' crate, they have to go out to find him; otherwise the mess at home will just get worse.

Still, Sally wonders if it's okay for the Cat to go out. "Sure," he cracks, "I'm an indoor/outdoor cat."

The writers wanted the stuff they made up to seem like Seuss might have

CONCEPT ART

ABOVE
Part of the challenge of bringing the Cat to the big screen was giving life to established sequences, such as the clean-up machine. The other half was devising new plot devices, like when Nevins the dog runs away (below) and subsequently moves the action outside.

created it. Contraptions like the Cat's vehicle, the S.L.O.W., (Super Luxurious Omnidirectional Whatchamajigger), for instance.

"We invented it, but when you see it in the film, and especially the way it looks, you don't necessarily think that it was something Seuss didn't do. That was very important to us," says David Mandel, another member of the writing team.

Once Myers was cast as the Cat, the screenplay started to get tailored towards his strengths. "He brings irreverence to the Cat," says Grazer. "So it's not purely a

benign children's tale. It's what Geisel probably would have done himself today because he was also irreverent."

Working with the writers, Myers was able to bring in all sorts of pop culture references and spoofs. The Cat does an Infomercial parodying the George Foreman grill, and mimics being an action movie hero. Fed up with chasing after the dog, he barks at him, "This time it's personal."

Grazer understood what the Cat was in the classic sense, but also had a vision of what he could be. He was hoping to add another dimension to the character, so that fifteen-year-olds would think he was cool, their parents would get the jokes, and five and six-year-olds wouldn't be offended.

"We are trying to reach everybody — fans and friends of the Cat and future fans and friends of the Cat."

B.G. SPINS   B.G. SPINS

CONCEPT ART   PULL NEVINS

Grinch Vs. Cat

Two classic Seuss characters, both with a unique story to tell

Quick, who would you rather be stranded on a desert island with, the Grinch or the Cat? Both of them would probably drive you crazy, but at least the Cat is good for a fun time. Until he has his change of heart, the Grinch is a real sourpuss.

Their story is also a lot different. The Grinch has more built in conflict. He goes from being crabby and mean to sweet and lovable. His character has to take a journey so he can appreciate the beauty of people and Christmas.

The Cat is an "elegant anarchist," as Grazer likes to call him. He stirs things up, he makes trouble, but he is not designed to undergo a great transformation. It's the kids who need to change.

So the Cat is just a catalyst. "To make it work as a movie, I had to create a starting point and an ending point for the Cat that

intersects with the kid's theme," says Grazer. "His role is to take the kids on an adventure so they learn something."

It's hard to say that a six-foot talking cat is more realistic than the Grinch, but the world he arrives in is our own. The Cat uses his Trans-Dimensional Transportolator as "kind of a doorway" from his world to this world.

While he's in Anville, the town where the kids live, things look sort of normal (until the portal opens). These are regular people wearing regular clothes on their back and driving cars. So what if there's a weird uniformity and everything is the same color? It's reality as we know it, more or less.

Whoville is, well, who knows? It is definitely outside our realm of experience. People don't look the same. In Whoville there were some 200 characters wearing

prosthetics; in Anville it's only the Cat and the Things.

"In the case of *The Grinch*, you have to try to imagine, 'How do people interact in Whoville?' and 'How afraid of the Grinch are they?'" says Grazer.

"That's a complete fantasy. Our arc is much more like 50% reality and 50% fantasy," says McDowell. The Cat is way more normal."

JIM CARREY IS

THE GRINCH

NOVEMBER 17

ABOVE
Actor Jim Carrey as the Grinch in *Dr. Seuss' How the Grinch Stole Christmas* took the film to a level of fantasy and make-believe way beyond *Dr. Seuss' The Cat in the Hat*. Unlike the Cat, he is the character who changes the most.

PARTY ANIMAL

Face it, without a Cat there is no movie. It's not called "The Kids and the Hat" or "The Mom and the Hat." It's *The Cat in the Hat*. The Cat *is* the story.

No wonder Bo Welch was sweating it. "If you're three months from shooting and you still don't know what the Cat looks like, you have a problem. We were down to the wire."

Three special effects makeup companies were auditioning for the job, which is common practice in Hollywood. Welch referred to it as the "bake-off."

It was basically a contest to see who could come up with the design everyone liked the best. In the course of three months, the filmmakers looked at test prosthetics, text makeup, wigs, fur, and whiskers for maybe 60 different versions of cats.

"The range of looks was astonishing, mind boggling," says Welch.

Finally, a decision was made to go with Steve Johnson's Edge FX. Johnson had done *Blade II* and *The League of Extraordinary Gentleman,* but for this one the meter was running. Whatever he came up with had to go through the approval gauntlet of the filmmakers, Mike Myers, Universal, Dreamworks, and Imagine.

"We had about eight weeks," says Johnson. "But in some ways it works better because everyone understands you have a goal and have to make a decision. I think the creative juices flow a little bit stronger and faster because of it."

The first question Johnson asked himself was, "how do you create a cat without putting a guy in a pair of pajamas and sticking a rubber nose on him?"

Johnson and his team played around with some realistic approaches, such as electrostatically flocking the whole face with soft fine fur. They also tried a tabby look that resembled a full-grown gray cat.

But Welch didn't want this turning into *Cats* on Broadway, so he steered towards a cleaner, clearer design. The look

became more graphic with sharp lines of black and white on the Cat's face, which fit the overall style of the film.

From there Welch, Johnson and Myers did endless refining. "Take a whisker away here, add one there, move the nose a quarter of an inch," recalls Welch. "It was exhausting, but if you don't have a close-up of a Cat you love, you're dead."

Welch saw the character as a lovable scoundrel and wanted that look reflected in the design. The way to get there was to allow Myers the freedom to use the expressiveness of his face.

"One of the great things about the makeup is that you still see me in it, I'm not entombed in plastic," says Myers. "It was the minimum amount of makeup that would suggest a Seussian cat."

Myers and Johnson pared down and started tearing away the face covering. "I looked at the way Mike's face moved when he smiled, when he smirked, when he raised his eyebrows, and designed the makeup smaller and smaller, thinner and thinner." says Johnson.

"Mike really knew what he was talking about," says Johnson. "So I went completely against what I normally would have done, which is show off my talents and design a full rubber mask. To hell with the actor," he laughs.

Together they worked out every aspect of the look. Where the white should end, where the hair should start and stop, how

to frame the face. They brought the face out wider with lines for more of a cat-like look. The one thing they couldn't fake was the long feline neck the Cat has in the book, so they put a stripe down the neck to make it look thinner.

"While it's true the cat has a feline body, he actually has a humanoid face, except for the snout, so it was all Operation Snout," jokes Myers.

"We used to keep all the snouts on the wall behind us like hunting trophies. So by the end of the movie there was like sixty snouts on the wall. I looked like a big game hunter, a Seussian big game hunter."

After dozens of tests on Myers stand-in, the Cat was finally ready to rumble.

TOP
Myers and Breslin prepare for a scene.

ABOVE
While hunting for Thing 1 and Thing 2 Conrad ends up catching himself.

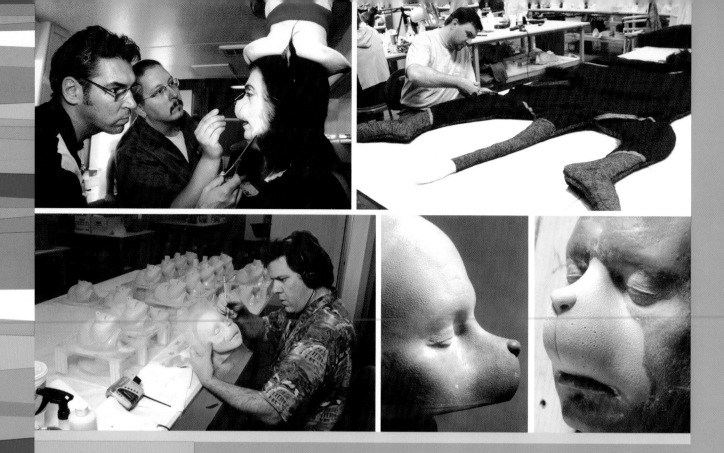

ABOVE

(above top left) Michael Smithson and Steve Prouty attend to some last minute trimming to Mike Myers. The whole makeup process took about three hours to apply.

(above top right) Ted Haines constructs an oversized cat suit for the Cat Rug effect. One of the most elaborate scenes, it was later cut from the final film.

(above left) James Rohland paints Thing appliances. Unlike the Cat makeup, which left much of Myers' face exposed, the Things were able to use a rubber full-face mask.

(above right) Forehead and muzzle appliances for the Cat's face. One of the goals of the makeup was to give Myers the freedom to use the expressiveness of his face.

"The first time I saw Mike in makeup, it made me feel high," says Welch. "You spend so much time and then it comes to life and you think, 'Oh, my god, there's the Cat in the Hat.'"

Every morning Myers would go into a zone for about three hours as the makeup was applied. "I didn't mind, you don't really notice it." he says.

"The hardest makeup I ever did was Fat Bastard, from the *Austin Powers* movies, that was five hours, sometimes seven. That makeup smelled like my hockey bag, and it was very hard to go to the bathroom in it. So this was very easy, in comparison."

Putting on his fur was a breeze next to the makeup process. Snaps and zippers could be easily hidden in his thick fur, and the upper and lower body parts were separate.

Fur suits, like the one for the Grinch, are often made of yak hair. The Cat was a blend of real human hair and angora

mohair, the soft belly hair of an Angora goat. The makeup team weeded though the hair by hand to find strands as soft as cotton to simulate the texture of a cat's coat.

"You can't just go out and buy fur, it has to be hand-woven of different lengths, one strand at a time," says Welch. "So you end up shooting endless tests of fur under different lighting conditions. It's just nutty."

"It was hard to make everyone happy with the look of the hair," adds Johnson. "We wanted to make sure it wouldn't go inky black on film so we had to introduce a lot of browns."

Three suits were made for Myers, all hand-tied on a Spandex leotard. It was an incredibly time-consuming process, much like making wigs.

The Cat was so well cared for, your poor tabby at home might feel jealous. He had a groomer on set and between shots he

Alec's Transformation

It wasn't simple turning a handsome guy like Baldwin into a slovenly mess. First step, Mark Garbarino paints a "Butt Chin" appliance for a make-up test (not used in the film). Meanwhile, Ted Haines constructs a fat suit to be worn by the actor under his wardrobe. Welch and Grazer were so used to the weirdness on the set that they hardly give a second look to Baldwin covered with purple ooze before a take.

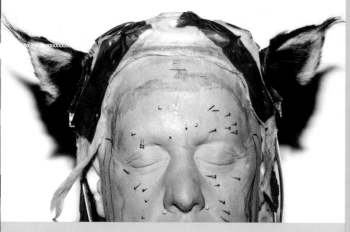

The finishing touch for the Cat suit was the ears, operated by motors hidden in a skull cap installed on Myers' head. But the motors were pretty noisy and weren't used in scenes with a lot of dialogue.

Cat

Edge FX put hours of hard work behind them in the quest for a perfect tail

would be constantly combed and brushed. Every morning each suit (about six all together) was freshened with an industrial dry-cleaning steamer that would re-flatten the hair, which was then combed out.

There were a few other flourishes applied before the Cat went off for a hard day's work. A skull cap containing motors for the ears was installed on the Cat's head. The ears could rotate four-ways manipulated by radio remote control.

"The only problem was that the motors were pretty noisy and went directly over Mike's cranium," says Johnson. "It drove him crazy. A lot of time when he had dialogue, we didn't operate the ears; his performance came first."

When all was said and done, by the end of the show, Johnson's crew had applied the Cat makeup over 300 times—to Myers, stunt performers and dance doubles.

Was it daunting? "You're asking me when it's almost done, so now I can say, 'Ah, it's easy. We do this kind of stuff all the time.' But come on, we could have ruined the whole movie," sighs Johnson.

If the Cat just dragged his tail around behind him, he would have been like another adored movie animal—the Cowardly Lion in *The Wizard of Oz*.

"It was great in that context, but in this film I think it would have infuriated the audience," says Johnson.

"In the beginning everyone was concerned about the hat and the face," he adds. "But I'm thinking if this tail doesn't work we're all going to look like idiots."

"The tail was an opportunity we didn't want to miss," agrees Welch.

Using the tail creatively was a way to enhance the Cat's performance. A white tuft was attached to the end so its movement would stand out. "It was sort of like Michael Jackson's silver glove. That's where the eye goes," says Johnson.

About eight different kinds of tails were designed. The one most widely used was a kinetic model where the movement of Myers' body just transferred to the tail through a series of properly weighted springs. It didn't require an operator, but it had a lot of life to it.

A more limp version of this style could be manipulated with mono-filament and a fishing rod attached to the tail. The rod was covered with green-screen fabric and then digitally removed. This one was used when the Cat wanted to tap someone on the shoulder with his tail.

Tales

A hand puppet model was also made. In this case, a very small performer could put his hand in the oversized tip of the tail and then grab anything. The arm was sheathed in green fabric where it exited the tail and was removed in post-production.

The cat suit had a built in battery pack in the belly and motors in the base of the tail to power a radio operated remote control tail. This one worked like flying a model airplane, and could spin in two directions in a kind of corkscrew motion.

"I was really pleased with that one because I knew the tail that would get on film was the one that was easiest and most comfortable to use," says Johnson.

It did have one drawback, however. "The problem with that one was we were hiding a

piece of mechanical equipment in the Cat's butt and there was a little bit of a noise factor," says Welch.

The most confining but incredibly versatile tail was the fully animatronic model. "This one could really do anything. It could reach up and pick the Cat's nose if we wanted it to," jokes Johnson.

This was activated by cables handled by two operators. The disadvantage was that Myers was tethered to wires running down his leg and out the bottom of his pants. The cables were again digitally removed or framed out of the picture.

All the tails were designed to come off easily so Myers could sit down as soon as the director yelled, "Cut." The tail could then be unclipped immediately. By who? The tail wrangler, of course.

ABOVE
Jeff Jingle and Bill Bryan test a cable controlled version of the tail. There was also a radio controlled tail and a kinetic tail, which was outfitted with springs and just bounced around with the movement of the Cat's body.

LEFT
A back view of the spandex undersuit with integrated cool suit and battery/wiring harness for the Cat's ear and tail motors. Positioned above the Cat's butt, the motor was a bit noisy to operate.

Alex McDowell, left, looks at designs with director Bo Welch.

Color My World

Production designer Alex McDowell gave the sleek futuristic look to *Minority Report* and the steely cold style to *The Fight Club*, but he says *The Cat in the Hat* is the most controlled film I've ever worked on, down to the last detail."

The tone and the look of the movie was crucial. A little bit too far one way and it's a comic book, a little bit too far the other way and it's unbelievable. Finding the right level of stylization was the key.

"You have to create a context for such a character to exist in," says Welch. "If you take a six-foot cat in a lovely hat and gloves and put him down in North Hollywood, it would be upsetting. You want it grounded in enough reality so it feels like it's happening."

The solution, unfortunately, wasn't to be found in the Seuss books. It's impossible to produce the Seussian world as it exists on the page because it's two-dimensional. You never actually see the Cat walk, for instance.

"If you literally take the book—houses with one window all rubbery and bent—then there's nothing to relate to," explains Welch. "It's plastic and completely artificial. What you want to do is create a world that is familiar and so people say, 'Oh, I want to go there.'"

What would it look like? "Bo and Alex solved the problem in a very sophisticated way with their palette and simplicity and repetition of shapes," says costume designer Rita Ryack. "It's very graphic, clean and clear. So it feels like a fairy tale world."

"Bo was a world-renowned production designer and he created the look of *Edward Scissorhands* and

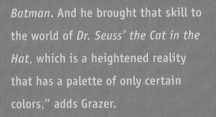

Batman. And he brought that skill to the world of *Dr. Seuss' the Cat in the Hat*, which is a heightened reality that has a palette of only certain colors," adds Grazer.

The Cat himself was the catalyst for deciding what colors to use. He's black and white and his hat is red and white. So those colors were reserved only for the Cat and the Things.

"We wanted the Cat to jump off the screen, so there are no Cat colors anywhere else," explains McDowell. "We decided on a limited palette that would create a lovely backdrop that was right on the edge of believability."

Blues, primary colors and pastels were tossed out. Greens and yellows were left to compliment the Cat.

"I started to collect fabric for the curtains and one of them caught the director's fancy," says set decorator Ann Kuljian. "It was a green striped material with daisies in it, and it became the starting point for other parts of the film."

After that discovery, everything just started coming up green and yellow. The wallpaper, the ice box , the storefronts downtown. Things were done to tweak the environment—furniture was slightly over-sized—but it's mostly the palette that strikes you.

The uniformity even carried over to the clothes. If red was the color of chaos, then Conrad was the closest with orange and yellow. Sally fit into the environment better with lavender and leaf green. And mom had a little of both with a hot pink.

"Typically in a movie you try to restrict your palette, so it doesn't get too confusing and become a big colorful mass," explains Welch.

The exterior of the houses was a soothing, if slightly odd lavender. It reminded Welch of the pastel suburban neighborhood he designed for *Edward Scissorhands*.

"That looked like a faded circus. People would say, how come no one paints their house this color? I thought it was nice for a movie but not to live in. It would make you nuts."

The Cat already is nuts. So the design and color scheme was heightened to reflect that fact. The story is resting on a cliff waiting to tip over into mayhem.

"When I started to work with him," recalls McDowell, "Bo said that on a scale of one-to-ten, if one is absolute reality and normal, and ten is absolute fantasy, we were starting at 4.5—and ending at 11."

"Top Cats"

Brian Grazer returns to produce more Seuss magic out of his movie hat

When producer Brian Grazer was wooing Theodor Geisel's widow, Audrey S. Geisel, to get the rights to *The Cat in the Hat*, a director of Dr. Seuss Enterprises. turned to Grazer and said, "You are the Cat in the Hat."

If working wonders on seemingly impossible productions and pulling miracles out of thin air makes you the Cat in the Hat, then Grazer is indeed the famous feline.

"For me it's critical that you get the foundation right. If you fail at that, the movie is going to be unfixable."

Brian Grazer, Producer

27

ABOVE
Bo Welch (seated), Brian Grazer and the kids watch a video playback of a scene.

good movie, it's almost like he can do any style of picture," says Alec Baldwin. "When you compare *Grinch* to *A Beautiful Mind* to *Ransom*, they're all different. It seems like he'll go anywhere with a camera."

The tireless Grazer, a onetime student at USC film school, is the kind of producer who is critically involved in the conception and the pre-production stage of filmmaking. "For me it's critical that you get the foundation right," he says. "If you fail at that, you can be on the set every step of the way and the movie is still going to be unfixable."

With Ron Howard, his partner in Imagine Entertainment, Grazer has produced over sixty movies and television series since 1982. He won an Academy Award® for Best Picture as producer of *A Beautiful Mind* in 2001. "If a producer has a recipe and he knows what makes a

Brian Grazer: Films and Television Work as Producer

- *The Alamo (2003)*
- *The Big House (2003) (TV)*
- *Intolerable Cruelty (2003)*
- *The Missing (2003)*
- *Dr. Seuss' The Cat in the Hat (2003)*
- *Arrested Development (2003) (TV)*
- *Miss Match (2003) (TV)*
- *Apollo 13: The IMAX Experience (2002)*
- *BS (2002) (TV)*
- *8 Mile (2002)*
- *Blue Crush (2002)*
- *Undercover Brother (2002)*
- *A Beautiful Mind (2001)*
- *24 (2001) (TV)*
- *Dr. Seuss' How the Grinch Stole Christmas (2000)*
- *Nutty Professor II: The Klumps (2000)*
- *Bowfinger (1999)*

- *Life (1999)*
- *EdTV (1999)*
- *The PJs (1999) (TV)*
- *Psycho (1998)*
- *Felicity (1998) (TV)*
- *Sports Night (1998) (TV)*
- *From the Earth to the Moon (1998) (TV Mini Series)*
- *Inventing the Abbotts (1997)*
- *Liar, Liar (1997)*
- *The Nutty Professor (1996)*
- *Ransom (1996)*
- *Fear (1996)*
- *Sgt. Bilko (1996)*
- *Apollo 13 (1995)*
- *The Paper (1994)*
- *My Girl 2 (1994)*

- *For Love or Money (1993)*
- *CB4 (1993)*
- *Boomerang (1992)*
- *HouseSitter (1992)*
- *Far and Away (1992)*
- *My Girl (1991)*
- *Backdraft (1991)*
- *Closet Land (1991)*
- *The Doors (1991)*
- *Kindergarten Cop (1990)*
- *Cry-Baby (1990)*
- *Parenthood (1989)*
- *Splash (1984)*
- *Night Shift (1982)*
- *Thou Shalt Not Commit Adultery (1978) (TV)*
- *Zuma Beach (1978) (TV)*

ABOVE
Grazer, Welch and Kelly
Preston (in hair and makeup)
in front a lavendar dog house
on the Simi Valley location.

Much of his attention goes to getting the philosophy of a film right before it starts. For *Cat* he knew he wanted to anchor it in reality. "It's a heightened reality, but it's a reality," he says. "Whereas *Grinch* isn't, that was a fantasy."

Dr. Seuss' How the Grinch Stole Christmas was the highest grossing film of 2000 ($260 million domestically), so he must have done something right. No matter how complicated *Grinch* was, Grazer says it taught him something. "I learned to embrace the problems and that obstacles are not insurmountable at all."

Since the Seuss books are so short, Grazer's main job as a producer was to imagine what they could be as a movie. "It takes a lot of studying or splitting of the atom," he admits. But it was worth it.

"Because they have universal themes, and because the illustrations ignite such fantasy in your mind as a child, it just leaves some sort of an indelible memory that is so positive," Grazer says.

"And so when I realized I had a chance to convert *The Cat in the Hat* or *How the Grinch Stole Christmas* into movies, I just was willing to do anything to do such a thing."

29

Bo Welch knows everything about creating cool worlds for movie fans

The way Brian Grazer sees it, he wasn't taking much of a risk hiring Bo Welch to direct *Dr. Seuss' The Cat in the Hat*. Welch had a distinguished career as a production designer but hadn't directed a film yet. "A lot of this is about creating a world," says Grazer, "and Bo is an expert at creating worlds."

Bo Welch's Credits as Production Designer

Men in Black II (2002)
What Planet Are You From? (2000)
Wild Wild West (1999)
Primary Colors (1998)
Men in Black (1997) *
The Birdcage (1996) *
A Little Princess (1995) *
Wolf (1994)
Batman Returns (1992)
Grand Canyon (1991)
Edward Scissorhands (1990) **
Joe Versus the Volcano (1990)
Ghostbusters II (1989)
The Accidental Tourist (1988)
Beetlejuice (1988)
The Lost Boys (1987)
Slow Burn (1986) (TV)
*Stark:
Mirror Image* (1986) (TV)
Violets Are Blue (1986)
Swing Shift (1984)
Heart of Steel (1983) (TV)

*Academy Award ° nomination
**BAFTA award for Best
Prooduction Design

Lots of them—all different. A frequent collaborator with Tim Burton, Welch fashioned the sleek surface of Gotham in *Batman Returns* and the unforgettable surrealism of *Beetlejuice*. For Barry Sonnenfeld, he designed the period romp, *Wild Wild West*, and the irreverent spoof *Men in Black*.

He's also excelled at creating character through environment in intimate films like Mike Nichols' *Primary Colors* and the gender bender *The Birdcage*.

"When you hire a director, you have to make sure he has the skills you want," says Grazer. "But you also have to make sure that the way he sees the world is exactly what you want because that's what will become the theme of the movie."

It was fitting, then, that he got his shot on *Dr. Seuss' The Cat in the Hat.* "Cat has been very important for me and my generation, and maybe not always in the best way," jokes Welch. "It instructed me how to have fun, but you have to know how."

While Welch was having fun as a production designer, he was preparing for his directing debut. "I met him when he was doing *Grand Canyon* for Larry Kasden ten years ago, and he knew he wanted to direct then," says Grazer.

Alec Baldwin, who plays the slovenly next-door-neighbor, first worked with Welch in 1988 on *Beetlejuice*. It was Baldwin's second movie.

"Everybody in the business knows what an incredible designer he is and how imaginative he is," says Baldwin. "So you knew it was just a matter of time before he directed movies."

Baldwin gives him high marks for his debut behind the camera. "Comedy needs to be played quickly, you want to stay ahead of the audience."

"We would do a take and he'd say faster. He knows what the movie is in his head, and there are a surprising number of people making movies who don't know that," laughs Baldwin.

Baldwin was happy to help Welch on his first film, and he wasn't alone. Much of the crew signed on because Welch was there. Costume Designer and Academy Award ° nominee Rita Ryack didn't have a burning desire to do the project until she heard who the director was going to be.

"I thought, wow, this might be a really great design collaboration. I knew he would have a strong point of view and that it would be cool, because Bo is cool."

Set decorator Anne Kuljian was also excited about the idea of working with a designer as a director. "Initially we thought we'd be working with another production designer, but he got out of that hat and just became the director," she says.

That's why he brought in a strong production designer in Alex McDowell (*Minority Report*, *The Fight Club*). "When I met Bo the first thing he asked me was, 'Can you do whimsy?'"

Although their approach was different—Welch came from an architecture background and McDowell from a painting background—their style seemed to compliment each other. Welch believes in paring down, while McDowell was always

adding layers. For *Dr. Seuss' The Cat in the Hat*, simplicity won out.

"Bo understood absolutely what we were trying to do visually and knew what he wanted visually, so we were able to go in a very straight line," says McDowell. "I think we were only able to make the schedule because of that."

Amidst all the chaos, Welch not only kept his vision but his childlike joy in creating a fantasy world. When a difficult location like the Simi Valley neighborhood came together, he experienced a combination of excitement over the scope of the movie and a soothing feeling that, "Hey this works."

"I'm always drawn to what happens when you make all the things come alive, and you can go down and touch it and walk around. That's what I love about making movies." ❦

FAR LEFT
Emanuel Lubezki, Welch, Breslin and Preston during the filming of the stairway luge scene.

ABOVE
"I think Bo is a genius," says Myers. "I'm just in awe of his vision."

BOTTOM LEFT
Welch created a relaxed set where everyone could throw ideas into the pot. From Left, Alex McDowell, Welch and Andy Lipschutlz.

Berg, Mandel & Schaffer Write Ferris Bueller meets Bugs Bunny

When producer Brian Grazer asked the writing team of Alec Berg, David Mandel and Jeff Schaffer who they might look to for inspiration in writing the screenplay for *Dr. Seuss' The Cat in the Hat*, they said, how about Ferris Bueller and Bugs Bunny? It must have been the right answer, because they got the job.

The writers had actually done uncredited work on *Dr. Seuss' How the Grinch Stole Christmas* for about a year, so they were well prepared for their Seussian adventure. "It was very flattering that Imagine and Universal came to us first on this," says Berg. "It was a big vote of confidence."

The guys first met at college where they worked together on the Harvard Lampoon. They were reunited as writers on Seinfeld in the early nineties. (Mandel did the famous *Bizzaro* episode.) Berg says Seinfeld's sometime slapstick tone was good training for The Cat. "It was about four juveniles," he quips.

Their main concern in doing the screenplay was being faithful to Dr. Seuss. "We're huge fans and we grew up with *The Cat in the Hat*, so we didn't want to disappoint ourselves," says Schaffer. "And we didn't want people going that's not *The Cat in the Hat*."

"We weren't going to cut to Tahiti or outer space. We tried to keep it in that world," adds Mandel.

When the three met with Grazer, they insisted that the structure for the movie was already there in the book. It had all the elements. Mom leaves, the Cat comes, makes a mess and cleans it up. The question was how do you turn a story that's sixty pages and mostly pictures into a ninety minute movie?

"We said, well, let's meet the kids, let's meet this family. Why is mom going out? And then how do we take one or two pages of mess and make that bigger and more fun? So we wound up just expanding the sections," explains Mandel.

Once they started writing they also borrowed some material from Seuss' sequel, *The Cat Comes Back*. From there they got the idea of spots that spread like measles—from the mother's white dress to the walls, to the rug, to the bed.

They also thought it would be fun to see the Cat dragging the kids into the outside world. And then when they do return home, the Seussian ooze is exploding along with the house. As crazy as it gets, it's all about the house and letting mom down.

It's a bigger version of what's in the book, but the new material is still part of the story because their adventure in town is connected to what's going on in the house.

At the same time, the writers wanted to create a film that parents could take their children to without having to poke out their own eyes. "Just because it's for kids doesn't mean it has to be stupid," says Mandel. "The *Simpsons* does it best. There are really smart jokes and then there are jokes the kids will enjoy."

The goal was to make a fun live-action cartoon where you could pull anything out of the hat, just like in the Bugs Bunny cartoons they admired as kids.

For them it was like *Ferris Bueller's Day Off* for kids.

"It's an unbelievable day in their life," says Berg. "They think they're stuck inside with this horrible baby sitter and this guy comes in and shows them the most fabulous time. It's really an incredible adventure."

Mike Myers adds the Cat to his menagerie of crazy characters

Mike Myers says he was born to play the Cat in the Hat, and who could argue with him? The irreverence, quick wit and lovability he displayed in *Wayne's World*, *Saturday Night Live*, and, of course, *Austin Powers*, are the very things that make the Cat the Cat.

ABOVE
The Cat may have planned the whole day but that doesn't mean things don't go wrong along the way. He and Conrad regroup in downtown Anville.

RIGHT PAGE
When all seems lost the Cat comes to the rescue, driving the cleanup machine into the house. That's just the kind of cat he is.

(Bottom right)
Back home, the Cat is tangled up in blue.

In Myers' childhood home near Toronto, Canada, the Cat had a Liverpool accent. His mother, a trained actress and native Liverpudlian, would read him stories. *The Cat in the Hat* was his favorite—and still is.

"Happiness to me was finishing my homework on Friday night, so I could enjoy myself for the rest of the weekend. And that's how I learned, it's fun to have fun, but you have to know how."

"I always loved the whole message of *The Cat in the Hat*," says Myers. "That anarchist kind of fun guy is a character I've wanted to play my whole life," he says.

But growing up, Myers was hardly an anarchist; he was closer in temperament to Sally, the good girl.

"I used to hang out with borderline juvenile delinquents, and I was always the kid saying, 'Come on, we are going to get

in trouble, eh, you don't want to do that.' But I also enjoyed their sense of fun."

Getting to play the Cat was like a childhood dream come true. His aunt in Liverpool worked in a place called Dinky Toys, and would send him stuff like the Panther Mobile from the animated *Pink Panther* TV show and James Bond cars.

"When I was a kid I was like, 'God, I would love to actually be in those cars.' And now I get to drive the Super Luxurious Omnidirectional Whatchamajigger [S.L.O.W.] and the Dynamic Industrial Renovating Tractormajigger [D.I.R.T.], that cleans up the house. So making the film was a very happy time for me."

All of those cartoons and comic books that are supposed to rot your brain as a kid, were put to good use by Myers. His performance as the Cat was inspired by other famous felines from pop culture.

There was Top Cat, who in turn was based on the fifties TV series, *The Phil Silvers Show*. And also Bert Lahr as the Cowardly Lion in *The Wizard of Oz*.

Myers also drew on "the cultural tradition, if you will, of anarchist animals," wild and woolly creatures like Bugs Bunny. "I always loved it when Bugs Bunny would put on a dress and be a girl bunny, and I got to do that," marvels Myers.

But the biggest influence in creating the personality of the fabulous feline comes from an unexpected source: Bruce Paltrow, Gwyneth's producer-director father who died in 2002.

ABOVE
"The ideas in the book are completely illustrated in the movie." says Myers.

"He was this warm, supportive, stubborn guy who would just come into your house and start telling you this needed to be done and that needed to be done," recalls Myers. "And you would go, 'Well, he is just so darn charming, I'm going to do it.'"

Don't tell anyone, but the Cat is based on just that kind of brash, self-confident and secretly sweet New Yorker. Coming from a reserved English-Canadian family, Myers

was instantly drawn to polar opposite New Yorkers when he first came to the city to be a part of *Saturday Night Live* in 1989.

He even married a New Yorker from Queens. "I don't know how people can be so opinionated, so outgoing and so lovable at the same time."

Myers may have had a strong vision of who the Cat is, but come the first day of shooting everyone on the set was wondering what he would pull out of his hat.

"Everybody was waiting up until the last minute," says Steve Johnson. "I mean, how do you play the Cat in the Hat? And the first couple of days on the set everyone was just in awe of what he was doing."

In reality, the transformation started months before for Myers. "It's a very interesting process being a guy who makes up characters," says Myers. "You begin by yourself and then shift the process and work

CAT

"Look, I'm a cat that can talk. That should be enough for you people."

Mike Myers as The Cat In The Hat

things out in front of hundreds of people. So there's no first day for me."

If he ever had any shyness about acting, he got over it on *Saturday Night Live*. With so little time and so many characters to play, there was no room for preparation.

"Acting is about overcoming your embarrassment," he says. When he's playing a role, "that's not really my home, that's not really my wife, that's not really my mother." And he's not really a cat.

Myers isn't a nervous performer, but he worried about making the right choices for the character, especially for a beloved icon like the Cat in the Hat. In moments of self-doubt, the support of the director and the crew was a welcome thing to have.

At times, Myers would bounce around the set filming a scene as the Cat, and at the end of the shot his momentum would land him up against a camera operator or electrician. "They'd say, 'Nice work,' or

'Great job.' I can't tell you how important that is."

Carrying not only the weight of the film, but the weight of the costume and the hat, everything was done to make Myers comfortable.

TOP
The Cat is a dude with a 'tude. Myers borrowed from the anarchy of Bugs Bunny

BELOW
The Cat comes off as a rascal, but he's there to help the Kids learn a lesson.

ABOVE
Tennis anyone? Among the things he can pull out of his hat are tennis balls.

The Cat costume even had a built in cooling system like the kind astronauts and race car drivers use. It's a vest with cold water circulating to help keep the body temperature down.

Myers used it mostly on location in Simi Valley where he had to stand around in the sun. As soon as a take was done, his tail was pulled off and he was hooked up to a refrigerator cable.

"He looked like a guy walking around with a cooler full of cokes behind him in lieu of a tail," cracked a crew member.

Back on the sound stages of Universal, it was easier to control the temperature.

Myers got the chills everyday when he went to work, but it was from the sets, the production design, the props and costumes.

"The trees are right out of the book,

and the sky is right out of the book," says Myers. "Bo and Alex and the whole team got together to re-create the feeling of having your mom or your dad reading you this movie."

Myers' job was to have fun with it. "You always had a sense that all of the logistical struggles were taken care of by the time the actors got to the set. All we had to do is play in that world."

And play they did. Myers not only got to be a human cat, but a cat in drag. And he loved seeing the joy in the kids' eyes as they bounced on the couch and did all sorts of flips.

He also loved being Carmen Miranda, but his favorite scene was when he plays a rasta protester who waves a petition at Alec Baldwin.

"The guy goes, 'I think it's really wrong, I think it's really wrong that trees are made of wood. I don't think a tree should have to be wood.' And I got to play that guy," says a delighted Myers.

Being the Cat clearly hit his silly bone. "My dad was a very silly father, so I grew up in a very silly house, and the Cat is silly in the best way.

The thing Myers admired about the Cat is that he's very cheeky. "If someone's talking and he gets bored, he just shows his boredom. And if he wants to say something stupid, he just blurts it out.

"And he is sarcastic at times, and then he is really sweet at other times. So there's a lot to do as the Cat. I enjoyed every minute of it."

TOP
"It was great to see the fun through Dakota and Spencer's eyes when we were bouncing on the couch," says Myers. "Dakota couldn't wait to do the flips. Frankly, I'm not nearly as adventurous as she is." The actors were attached to wires to get the bounce necessary for this scene.

ABOVE
"Stick with me and everthing will work out," the Cat tells the skeptical kids.

43

"Cat People"

Spencer Breslin's just a cat who wants to have a good time

At the age of eleven, Spencer Breslin already has an impressive acting resume. He's been in ten movies including *Santa Clause 2* with Tim Allen and the upcoming *Raising Helen* with Kate Hudson. He's even produced a documentary about being in the *The Kid*.

44

ABOVE
Breslin and Fanning are not hunting for butterflies; they're trying to catch the Things.

"Spencer's got a lot going on," says his film mom, Kelly Preston. "He's writing scripts and he's directing things. He's a little man in this smaller body."

"Spencer is like the smartest person of any age I've ever met in my life," says Myers.

As Conrad in *The Cat in the Hat*, Breslin is the kind of kid who gets into everything. When he stages a stunt he calls "indoor stair luge," sliding down the staircase on a cookie sheet with a metal pot for a helmet, his sister Sally just adds it to the lengthy list of "Conrad's serious errors in judgment." (She's a bit of a priss and the exact opposite of her brother.)

As his mother leaves the house, she begs him to not make a mess because she's having a party for her important clients that night. Don't bet on it.

"He's a great kid but he only knows how to have too much fun. So he can strike havoc on the house when he wants to," says Breslin.

Between Conrad's chaos and Sally's fastidiousness, the house is way out of whack. That's where the Cat comes in.

His job is to balance the scales of fun and rules.

"You may think the Cat is just a mischievous guy, but he's there to give families a better life," says Breslin.

Part of the kick of making movies is getting to do stuff you normally couldn't get away with, like turning the living room sofa into a trampoline and, of course, the luge scene.

"I get all this weird Seussian padding on: pillows, stuffed animals, bread, marshmallows, kitchen supplies, anything you can name, I've got it on," he says. "They had the cookie sheet on a metal rack at the top of the stairs and it curves around and I'm going down 10-15 mph. It was exactly like a roller coaster!"

Is this something Breslin would like to try at home?

"Never, never. I would never dream of doing anything like that," he laughs, although he admits to sharing some of Conrad's mischievousness.

Breslin has lived in New York all his life and can't imagine ever leaving. "It's home, home is home." But he also feels

totally at ease on the set. (It must run in the family: his younger sister Abigail played Mel Gibson's daughter in *Signs*.)

Perhaps preparing for his next career as a director, Breslin does a hilarious imitation of cinematographer Emanuel Lubezki (affectionately known as Chivo) setting up a shot on the set.

"'Bo, the shot is beautiful! You know Barkley, the lighting is not good, Zimmerman, put me in focus. Bo, the shot is a disaster. Wait, no, no, it is beautiful, it is beautiful, Bo!'"

ABOVE TOP
Conrad can't keep his hands out of anything, including his mom's fresh baked cookies.

ABOVE
The Cat tries to convince the Kids they're going to have a good time, but they're not so sure.

Dakota Fanning

is the picture perfect brain of the house

"**P**eople ask me who's the greatest actress I've ever worked with," says Alec Baldwin, "because I've worked with all these great actresses—Nicole Kidman, Demi Moore, Jennifer Jason Leigh. And now my new answer is Dakota Fanning. Dakota Fanning is the greatest actress I've ever worked with."

ABOVE
Sally gets her head examined by the Cat's Phunometer. It says she's a control freak.

TOP RIGHT
The Cat takes Sally and Conrad for a ride in his car: she even gets to drive.

He's not kidding.

"This kid is incredible. She's so spot on and plays her intentions through the lines," adds Baldwin. "Both of the kids are great. They are not child actors, they are actors."

It's not surprising that the nine-year-old Fanning has been planning her career for years. Since she was a little kid, she would play at being her mother and little sister around her house in Conyers, Georgia. At eight she was the youngest actress ever nominated for a Screen Actors Guild award for her role as Sean Penn's daughter in *I Am Sam*. In 2003 she was in *Uptown Girls* and in 2004 she stars in Tony Scott's *Man of Fire* with Denzel Washington.

In *The Cat in the Hat*, her character, Sally, spends a lot of time with her PDA plotting out her life for the next fifty years. Everything is perfect about her— her hair, her purple and green dress, and her grades.

She can definitely be a pain sometimes. Her relationship with her brother isn't that great.

"Do you know how hard it's getting to tell people we're related?" she says in the movie. Obviously they have some stuff to work out.

"I'm so uptight that I don't get invited to my best friend's birthday party because she wouldn't let me be head chef," Fanning says about her character.

"I said if you're not going to let me be head chef, I'm not going to be your friend anymore."

When Sally and the Cat and Conrad look in at the party and see how much fun everybody is having, it proves to be a turning point for her. "Sally learns, 'Well, maybe I'm being too mean.' That scene is sort of Sally's lesson right there."

At first she doesn't like the Cat, but then loosens up and learns how to have some fun too. On this film, learning how to have fun was pretty easy. For a scene when the kids use the sofa as a trampoline, the actors had to go to stunt school for a whole month. "We got on bungees and did back flips and front flips and we bounced on our head. So that scene in the movie, that's us doing it," says Fanning.

In real life, Fanning got along with Breslin a lot better than Sally does. "We did everything together. We went to lunch

and rode to the set in the golf cart. It was really nice."

"Dakota is so sweet that it was all I could do not to bite on her head because she is so incredibly cute," says Myers. "I just wanted to gnaw on her head, I didn't want to break skin, just gnaw." 🎤

ABOVE
Sally doesn't like surprises so she plans the rest of her life on her PDA.

"Cat People"

Alec Baldwin is right at home playing the heavy as an all-new character

Alec Baldwin plays the not-so-good neighbor, Lawrence Quinn, one of the new characters invented for the film. More accustomed to being a heroic, sexy figure in films like *The Marrying Man* and *The Shadow,* Baldwin had a great time playing a comedic character in *Dr. Seuss' the Cat in the Hat.*

ABOVE
Quinn (Baldwin) isn't the good guy he pretends to be. He's trying to get Spencer sent away to military school so he can have his mother all to himself.

"What's fun about Quinn is that he's totally not what he pretends to be," says Baldwin. "When he goes home, he takes off his girdle and he's got this enormous gut and he's just a complete slob. He presents himself as being sophisticated and caring, but he's really a big fat pig."

Kids will no doubt squeal with delight at the scene where Quinn picks the lint out of his blubbery belly button.

Quinn makes a big show of his affection for the kids, but secretly he's trying to get their mom to break up the family and send her son Conrad (Spencer Breslin) off to military school. The kids instinctively know he's a phony; Joan has to find out for herself.

"That's a classic thing in comedy, where the kids have the ability to smell out a rat or in this case a pig," says Baldwin.

Baldwin plays Quinn as a pathetic character who the Cat gets to humiliate.

"The good thing when you do a movie like this is you can almost get away with anything," he says. "You get to express yourself in really operatic ways, you scream and shout and whine and cry. It's the kind of acting that would be bad acting in a more naturalistic setting."

"Cat" was also a chance for Baldwin to be funny for a change. "Alec is absolutely hilarious in this movie," says his costar Preston. "It doesn't matter what he's doing in the scene, he's just so amusing. He's the bad guy in the film, but he's such a playful and generous actor to work with."

Baldwin had to shoot a number of scenes with the family dog, who is constantly running away. Actors often hate playing opposite kids and animals (think W.C. Fields), but Baldwin maintained a sense of humor about the whole thing.

"I don't like any performers who are treated more affectionately than I am. That dog had two people with it every minute, feeding it, stroking it, it's really kind of sickening," he says, tongue firmly planted in cheek.

But Baldwin loved working with the kids. "If you asked them to do a scene fifty times, they would do it. They have a boundless passion for acting and it's very infectious."

Breslin returns the compliment. "Alec is just the opposite of that character he plays. He's the nicest guy in the world."

"That's a classic thing in comedy, where the kids have the ability to smell out a rat or in this case a pig"

Alec Baldwn,
on his character, Quinn

ABOVE
Finally Quinn gets what he deserves—a bath in a river of purple Seussian ooze.

LEFT
Quinn is allergic to cats, and that's only for starters. This Cat is going to make him really sick.

"Cat People"

Kelly Preston plays the perfect mom with a soft spot for Lawrence

Kelly Preston has appeared in a lot of movies (*What a Girl Wants, For Love of the Game, Addicted to Love*), but nothing got her two kids as excited as when she told them she was going to be in *Dr. Seuss' The Cat and the Hat*.

TOP
The Cat has a bit of a crush on the mom. "She is a good-looking gal. I'm not gonna lie to you," says Myers, while goofing on the set in this off-camera moment.

TOP RIGHT
Joan begged Conrad to keep the house clean for the big party that night. Fat chance!

BOTTOM RIGHT
Joan offers her guests a delicious purple cupcake from the Cat's Kupkake-inator.

"Literally they were jumping up and down," she says. "And my daughter Ella does all the Cat's lines. She calls him 'de cat'n de hat.'"

Preston plays the single mother of two kids. In the Dr. Seuss book, we see only her foot as she returns home to ask her children the famous question: "What did you do today?" In the film, her role is considerably expanded. She's now a real estate agent who is having a very important party at the house that night. So the kids really have to keep it clean.

Her son Conrad "is just nuts and will try anything" and her daughter Sally is "very controlled and precise." Their mother is somewhere in between.

"She's a combination of the two kids," says Preston. "Joan is a little offbeat, which I love, and Bo let me play her that way."

Joan is living partially in the reality of being a working mother and balancing a lot of stress and trying to keep her family in one piece. But this being "The Cat in the Hat," she's also simultaneously living in a different, crazier world.

"I get to heighten reality and sort of push off the edges a little bit with my character. I mean, look where we live. So there's a little extra sense of other things going on as well."

Yeah, like a six-foot talking cat. Yet for the story to work there has to be a level of believability. "Every aspect of the movie has to be on the money, so, of course, you have to have the dream girl leading lady, and Kelly is definitely the dream girl leading lady," says Baldwin.

Joan thinks that Quinn is a great guy who's going be her knight in shining armor, which he most definitely is not.

"Joan is a little offbeat, which I love, and Bo let me play her that way."

Kelly Preston

"Joan is very open minded and sympathetic towards people, so she is perhaps more patient and kind to Quinn than she should be," says Baldwin. "She sees things about him that don't read all that correctly. But in the end, even Joan catches on to him."

Amy Hill muses about her on-screen life in the Cat boat seat

Probably no character in movie history has slept through her role and accomplished more for the film than Amy Hill in *Dr. Seuss' The Cat and the Hat*. Hill plays Mrs. Kwan, Sally and Conrad's babysitter.

In Dr. Seuss' original story, written in 1957, the kids were left home alone and it didn't seem to matter. Today that would seem irresponsible on the part of the mother, so Mrs. Kwan was invented for the story. At the same time she's an ideal comic foil.

For starters there's her appearance. Coke-bottle glasses cover most of her face, lavender pin curls, and an out-of-it expression as she shuffles into the house. And that's about as lively as she gets.

Mrs. Kwan is not a very good baby sitter, and literally sleeps through most of the movie. "I come in, sit down, turn on the TV, and fall asleep," says Hill. "But I'm not just lying there, I'm very busy."

There's the time the Cat plops down on her on the sofa. "This is the lumpiest couch I've ever sat on," he grouses. And then when he sees what it is, demands to know, "Who is this dreadfully uncomfortable woman?" So the Cat takes her, puts her on a hanger and hangs her in the closet. And she just keeps snoring.

"Bo and I spent long hours over late night lattes talking about how it was important for the children out there to know Mrs. Kwan isn't dead," recalls Hill. "So I've never learned so many ways to snort and snore and shout out. She's just a crazy character."

One of Welch's improvisations during shooting was to have Hill dream she is at a card casino and shouts out to the dealer, "hit me."

"It's not explained and yet it's hysterically funny," says Welch. "What else can you do when you're sleeping? That was really fun to do."

Hill's wildest scene was undoubtedly after the Things take over and turn the house into a chaotic Seussian theme park. She actually becomes a flume ride and the kids and the Cat sit on her and ride her down a river of purple ooze. Most of it was done with an over-sized fiberglass model and CGI, but she was in on some of the action, still sleeping, of course.

The good news was that Hill, who has worked on films like *Big Fat Liar* and *Lilo and Stich*, didn't have a lot of lines to memorize. "Of course I didn't consider that I was going to be doing so many stunts either," she laughs.

Sean Hayes plays a simple fish who's in a little too deep

In "The Cat in the Hat," Sean Hayes started out as a fish and became a person. Actually, Hayes, the costar of TV's *Will and Grace*, has two roles in the film. He is the voice of reason as the kids' talking fish. Later, he was cast as their mother's supercilious boss, Mr. Humberfloob, owner of Humberfloob Realty.

The talking fish is one of the great innovations in the book. In the film, the fish's role is expanded thanks to the creativity of the filmmakers and CGI. The fish now gets to go outdoors and be a part of the big adventure.

So how did Hayes become a fish? "I was walking down the street and ran into Ron Howard, [whose company produced the film]. He said, 'You look like a fish.' And I said, 'You look like an actor I used to know.' So I read the script and loved it."

"The fish is kind of the catalyst who always reminds the audience why these kids need to behave, that the mother is coming back home for a party," says Hayes. "The fish is like the parent when the mom goes away."

In this off-center world, it's totally accepted that fish can talk. "One of my favorite lines is when Sally says, 'The fish is right.' That line just makes me laugh because it says that she has accepted the fish into her life as a talking, functioning thing," adds the actor.

This is only the third time Hayes has done voice work, but he found the job fun without being too taxing. "It's nice, you don't have to dress up," he jokes. "It's a terrific, easy gig for an actor."

"It's like a tennis match. The animators will animate for your voice, and then sometimes you'll dictate to the animators. So it's a wonderful collaborative thing."

Since the fish grows increasingly alarmed about what's going on as things spin further and further out of his control (he is only a fish after all), Hayes decided to play the character with a frantic, urgent quality to his voice, "always screaming and real high. It just sounded funnier."

Hayes recorded the part against a white screen, without the benefit of seeing what the fish looked like in front of him. "I joked with Bo that it would be easier as an actor if I dressed up as a fish to say the lines."

He had no trouble, however, getting into the Humberfloob role. The voice was the key thing. "I liked using the lower register and leaning into my 'r's.' It made a man who is very controlling and somewhat flawed (if having a germ fetish wasn't flawed enough)," jokes Hayes.

welcome
to the
neighborhood

CONCEPT ART

CONCEPT ART

CONCEPT ART

THIS PAGE
Early on Welch sketched a house the way a kid might do it. It became a model for the Kids' neighborhood where everything looks the same. Things may seem almost normal but then the Cat comes.

(below) Welch wanted to create a Seussian sky like the kind you see in the books. With the help of CGI, the sky wound up looking very much like this early illustration. The neighborhood reminded Welch a little bit of the one he created for "Edward Scissorhands."

The neighborhood where the Cat comes to visit and wreaks havoc was one of those rare movie locations that everyone loved. It was fun, it was magical, it was Seussian.

The production had been hunting all over the country for the perfect place to use as the idealized community of Anville (in the book the town doesn't have a name). The director was looking for a vaguely nostalgic, old-fashioned place that was free from the problems of the real world. No wonder they had trouble finding it.

Location scouts checked out an abandoned Naval base in Southern California, but it would have taken too much work to fix it up. They needed rolling green hills with a minimum of landscaping and nothing on the horizon.

Finally, they decided they would have more control if they built a set close to home in Simi Valley, California, a sprawling residential area 45 minutes north of Los Angeles. They took over 13 acres of ranch land and made "a little paradise."

"We mowed all the hills, irrigated and watered forever, sowed it with meadow grass and created our neighborhood" says McDowell.

The model for the house was a classic child-like drawing Welch did with a peaked roof, a door in the middle, a window on each side, and a chimney. They wanted the feel of a picture-perfect American small town with rows of houses and picket fences, the kind of idealized look you'd see

CONCEPT ART

ABOVE
The unusual look of the trees and plants was inspired by the stuff in the Seuss books. Most of the trees and bushes in the film were fake, a combination of four different kinds of leaves and flowers to create a Seussian mix.

in turn-of-the-century paintings by Grant Wood and Grandma Moses. "The accumulated effect of these ridiculous, almost toy-like houses was really nice, it was a fun set to be on," adds McDowell.

Working over a hurried sixteen weeks, a crew of 250 built the exteriors of 24 lilac-colored houses, put in roads, and poured the concrete. About six of the houses were complete and all of them had a frontyard and backyard. This is where Sally, Conrad and you-know-who go skulking around looking for their lost dog, Nevins. The street was lined with hundreds of odd plants and lollipop-shaped trees modeled after the goofy growth in the Seuss books. When it was done, the look was incredible.

"When we drove out to the ranch and came over the last bluff and there's this dirt road and all these lilac-colored houses, it was a lovely feeling, like, 'Oh, I just want to go down there and walk around,'" says Welch.

It all looked so inviting from the distance that people driving by on Highway 118 would call the local realtor to inquire about this new development.

And the strangest thing happened, people loved coming to work. "Bo said that with this set we created a wonderful drug that changed people. As they went through the location they got all happy and started walking slower and looking around sort of dreamily,' marvels McDowell.

Kids, of course, felt right at home on the set. When McDowell brought his

ABOVE
Judging by the look of the location, the kids could be living in the fifties or the present. The neighborhood of lavender houses built on 13 acres of ranchland in Southern California gave the story the timelessness it needed.

RIGHT
Welch watches as the "little paradise" is prepped for shooting. "We needed to come up the hill to the house and for it to be in the right light," he says. The road and rows of houses were plotted in the computer and then constructed on the set.

OPPOSITE PAGE
A crew of 250 built 24 lilac-colored houses, creating from scratch the idealized Seussian community of Anville on the rolling ranch lands of Simi Valley, 40 minutes north of Los Angeles.

six-year-old daughter, she immediately started running up and down the hills. "It was built for her and she knew it. I think that's an indication of how much kids are going to like this film."

The other great set was a three block stretch of antique shops and quaint stores in the Old Town section of Pomona, Calif., a small city east of L.A., transformed into downtown Anville. Welch thought of it as Main Street in a western with the Cat riding into town to save the day—or not.

In the center of the town was a giant anvil, and everything spread out from there. Storefronts on the street were simplified and painted over in the distinctive green and yellow palette of the film. So everything looked nice and clean

and uniform, like a timeless place. Taking a kids-eye view, Welch identified all the stores only with signs and no words. So a hot dog stand had a big neon hot dog in front, a ice cream parlor had a big ice cream cone and a coffee shop had a big coffee cup.

The stores remained open for business as they were being painted and traffic continued on the street as it was primped for shooting. Local residents would come by to have a look at the miraculous changes to their town. The only incident reported was

ABOVE
What's a kid to do? As the Cat's world seeps into our world, everything changes dimension. The living room looks like a fun house. Flowers on the wallpaper come off the walls and the phone is enormous.

ABOVE RIGHT
This is what happens when you have too much chaos in your life. As a tornado escapes from the Thing's crate, Conrad stuggles to keep his sister out of the vortex. The Cat is calm in the eye of the storm.

a fraternity prank when a bunch of college kids stole the neon golf tee from the golf shop, but it was returned the next day.

McDowell and his team of wizards succeeded in creating what Mike Myers called "a universe that exists and doesn't exist."

"It has to be grounded in some kind of reality but it has to be cartoon-like enough to contain a story where a six-foot cat can come into your home," laughs Welch.

The bounds of reality were literally stretched when shooting moved to the Universal Studios stage 28 for the interiors of Sally and Conrad's house. This was one of the most important sets because most of the story takes place in the rooms of the house. Everything was tweaked a little. Set decorator Ann Kuljian made the windows a little larger than

normal, the furniture bigger and even door knobs were over-sized to give a slightly disorienting quality. And then the Cat comes and things get crazier and crazier.

Once Thing 1 and Thing 2 get loose in the house, nothing is ever the same. It becomes what the Cat calls the "too-much-fun house," a staging ground for chaos. With just one touch, the walls fall away and the kids are standing on the precipice of a wild Seussian landscape. For this, an entirely different set was created on stage 12, the largest on the lot. It was one of the most complicated locations McDowell had ever worked on.

Designers took the straight lines of the original house and literally stretched them in the computer using an elaborate 3-D program. There were too many dimensions, to create this stuff on paper.

Preliminary

For months the house was distorted and pulled inside the computer. After that, about 250 blueprints were printed out and a very skilled team of sculptors constructed foam models. There wasn't a straight line in sight so there was no place to take a conventional measurement.

The result is almost unrecognizable, but with elements of the real house floating around—a window frame here, a piece of the staircase there, a bit of molding. The furniture is twisted up like pretzels, the telephone is twice the size and flowers come off the wallpaper.

"It's as if we turned the house into wax and melted it," says McDowell.

"This was a very complicated computer-driven piece of architecture. It's full of extremely elaborate forms and shapes, but in the end by painting it very simple colors,

ABOVE
As poor Sally discovers, the Thing's crate is no ordinary box—it's the Cat's Trans-Dimensional Transportolator— kind of a portal between his world and ours. Once Spencer lets the Cat out of the bag, everything goes topsy turvy.

ABOVE
Okay, the Things are back in the crate and the house seems to be back to normal when suddenly the roof caves in and the walls collapse. The original set, still standing on stage 28, was trashed to film the house collpasing.

BELOW RIGHT
The house as it looked in an early conceptual drawing right as it's opening into the Seussian landscape. After that, the house was distorted and pulled inside a computer for months before the final design was created.

it ends up looking like a children's illustration," explains McDowell.

After this heady experience, the crew headed back to the original house still standing on stage 28. By now the Things have been put back in their crate and order seems to have been restored, when suddenly the whole house collapses from being stretched this way and that. For anyone who wanted to vent a little frustration after 15 weeks of shooting, this was a great opportunity.

"We took chunks out of the walls and dismantled the set," says Kuljian. "We destroyed all the furniture. We had plaster and pipes coming out of everywhere."

"The whole staircase was destroyed," adds McDowell. "So when you see the stuff

falling [on screen] from the upstairs to the downstairs, it was really falling."

The beauty of all the locations and what makes them so much fun is that they had one foot in a recognizable reality no matter how weird things got.

"It's an invitation into a great world where you can let your imagination run wild and you are not restrained by the laws of physics," crows Welch.

CONCEPT ART

CONCEPT ART

ABOVE
After their house is trashed, Sally and Conrad try to restore order by getting the Things back into the box they came in. It's a little late for that, isn't it?

LEFT
Creating the "too much fun" house was one of the most complex sets McDowell had ever worked on. The laws of physics and logic no longer applied. "It's as if we turned the house into wax and melted it." he says.

BOTTOM
The design for the chaos house was too wild with too many dimensions to be created on paper. Designers took the straight lines of the original house and literally stretched them in the computer using a state-of-the-art 3D program.

CATS AT WORK

It's one of the accepted bits of wisdom in the film business that you should never work with animals and children. So not only was Bo Welch a first-time director, he had to handle kids, a dog and a cat that talked. None of these factors in itself would have been a problem, if it didn't create a massive scheduling puzzle that only Einstein—or a great assistant director — could possibly figure out.

ABOVE
"It was great getting up and seeing what Bo had created that day." says Myers.

BELOW
Director-in-training Spencer Breslin and Dakota Fanning yell action.

"Scheduling was the most daunting part of the movie," admits Welch. "It took Mike three-and-a-half hours to put on his makeup. Meanwhile, the kids, who were nine and eleven, legally only had a certain amount of hours they could work, and we had to schedule in their school time. So to get overlap when Mike was in his prime and the kids were in their prime was really hard."

The Cat and the kids were in most scenes together so it took some sleight-of-hand to shoot when they couldn't be there at the same time. "You end up using Cat doubles and then kid doubles. You use kid doubles late at night and shoot over their shoulder or put them in the background. It worked," explains Welch.

Once production got under way in September, 2002 on stage 28 of the Universal Lot, there were the usual crises that are part of life on a movie set. "Changes come constantly, and that's a big part of our job," says prop master

Robin Miller. "An actor maybe doesn't like the color of something or mechanically something doesn't work. Or the director may say, I want something else at the last minute. Whatever we planned five months ago doesn't matter. In five minutes we need something totally different."

Welch actually enjoys that part of the process. "It's a wild scramble but it's also exhilarating because you get into the military feel of a movie company, racing around and solving problems."

No matter how much money you spend to control the environment, filmmaking is always at the mercy of the weather, as Welch found out in Simi Valley. It was early fall and with a desert climate, there shouldn't have been a problem. Guess what?

TOP
In the chaos house, Welch created an environment for the Cat and the Kids to play in.

ABOVE
Almost in character, Breslin clowns around on the set while Fanning watches.

ABOVE

A Seussian street in Old Town Pomona conjured up by production designer Alex McDowell. A hammer marks the hardware store, a cone the ice cream shop, and a hot dog the fast food joint.

BELOW

After running a red light with the Kids in the car, the Cat crashes the S.L.O.W. in downtown Anville in an early drawing. When it came time to shoot the scene, rain delayed filming for a day.

The production was scheduled to be there for three weeks, but most mornings the fog was so thick you couldn't see six-feet front of you. It was day-after-day of soup.

Welch says, "We had twenty acres of lilac houses and you'd pull up and say, 'Where's the set?'"

They tried tightening up the shots until the fog burned off, but even then it was a lot darker than they expected. "The set was gray and what I wanted was sunny and beautiful," says the director. "So it was a source of real nail-biting."

How did they solve it? If you look closely at the finished film you'll see a lot of shots where the sky has been replaced with a CGI effect. "We put in a blue Seussian sky with swirling clouds, and lightened it up to create a more pleasant

mood," says Welch. "We planned on doing this anyway, but not to this extent."

Scheduling and weather had a hand in derailing a car mishap that takes place in Old Town Pomona. After the Cat drives the S.L.O.W. through a red light, the car slams into a statue and comes to a stop in an intersection. A second, damaged car had been built for the shot and was rolled out and set up in the middle of the street.

Just as the company arrived at the location to shoot, the sky darkened and it started raining. The car couldn't be left out overnight on what was normally a busy business street. So the set had to be undressed and then reassembled all over again the next day.

Problem solving and thinking on your feet are pretty much a way of life on movie sets. For instance, there's a scene where the

CONCEPT ART

ABOVE
Early conceptualizations of the neighborhood. It took 250 people sixteen weeks to build the actual set as seen above the sketch.

LEFT
A sequence of shots showing a Cat's eye view of the community where the kids live. It looks peaceful from the distance but it's not going to stay that way for long.

79

ABOVE
To create downtown Anville, the production took over three blocks of shops in Old Town Pomona. The set was modeled after a combination of Universal CityWalk and an ancient Japanese shopping street.

BELOW
Ted Haines prepares to test the Inflating Cat Suit on Jason Hamer. The suit inflated with a rush of hot air from four industrial vacuum cleaners.

Cat drinks some milk when he shouldn't -- he's lactose intolerant. He blows up like a balloon. No one quite knew how they were going to pull this off, and time was running out.

"I think every department on this film was a nervous wreck about doing the expansion gag on Mike. It's potentially dangerous," says Steven Johnson, who designed the Cat's makeup.

Inflating him with 8000 pressurized pounds in maybe two seconds was a scary proposition. The Cat basically had to blow up like a ten-foot beachball. "Special effects refused to do it and the digital people felt it

was too much expansion for digital work," adds Johnson.

So one night Johnson got the idea of blowing up garbage bags using four industrial vacuum cleaners and reversing the air flow. "We blasted it full of air and it just got bigger and bigger. "I just cracked up and thought this is going to be great as long as it doesn't hurt Mike."

An elastic cat suit was hastily made and the shot went off without a hitch—a last minute innovation that worked.

Unexpected things were always happening on the set. In one scene the Cat has to hide from a bunch of kids at a

Cakes

birthday party, so he hangs from a tree and pretends to be a piñata. The kids start flailing away at him, having a great old time, shouting "piñata! piñata!"

"They were just hitting him harder and harder and one of the kids starts screaming, 'he's breaking!'" recalls Johnson. "And I'm thinking, I don't remember that line in the script. And then the piñata swings around slowly and they've beaten his tail off. The wires and motors were coming out. They weren't ad-libbing."

Being on the set wasn't all work and no play. Cinematographer Emanuel Lubezki (nicknamed Chivo) delighted in watching Myers do his thing. "It was fun to watch a comedian go insane in front of you and create things that weren't scripted, and just be clever and funny," he says. "I kept thinking, how many people would pay me to be here?" 🎙

ABOVE
The kids search for their dog in Anville.

Left
"Look, I'm not a big rules guy," the Cat tells Spencer, "but this is my one: No opening the crate. No lookee, no touchee. Got it?" Which, of course, is an offer Spencer can't refuse.

IT'S A BIRD, IT'S A PLANE, IT'S A CAT!

On some movies you can show up the day of the shoot and wing it. *The Cat in the Hat* was not one of them. Because of the complex marriage of live and computer action with animatronics and puppeteering, everything had to be meticulously planned in advance.

42 CONT.

SCENE 48

SCENE 48B

Action sequences like the famous cleanup and the iconic Cat juggling scene might look complete on screen but were filmed in tiny, tortuous pieces. "We shot for months without having ever completed a scene. So you have to think things through ahead of time," says Welch.

Forward thinking was assisted by a new computer pre-visualization software called Softimage SXI that is revolutionizing how films are put together in Hollywood.

What it does is convert story boards into a digital format, and then puts in the characters, which allows the director to see how the whole thing is going to fit together.

"I encouraged Bo to do this because it helps you pre-visualize the movie," says cinematographer Emanuel Lubezki.

"It was a great tool for me because I could talk to Alex in advance about how I wanted to light a set."

McDowell had actually used "previz," as it's called, on Seven and Minority Report, so he was all for it. "It's enormously helpful for the really complex things where you have many departments interacting," he says.

Building sets and blocking scenes, like the film's complicated opening shot where a remote controlled cable cam swoops in over the rooftops right up to the front door peephole, were simplified and streamlined using previz.

The move to Old Town Pomona was also pre-vsiualized so the cam operator knew where to put the cables. The information from previz was converted into camera

moves, saving time and money. "It's very cheap actually," says McDowell.

Anything to make life easier was welcome, especially for the scene where the Cat has his great moment from the book—juggling a rake, a cake, an umbrella and a fishbowl, all while balanced on a large rubber ball.

If that wasn't already a ten on the cinematic scale of difficulty, it was decided fairly late in the day to add a song leading up to the balancing act. "Singing and dancing are in Mike's cinematic DNA," says Grazer. "People love to see him dance."

So a song was written by multiple Academey Award ® nominee and Tony winner (*Hairspray*) Marc Shaiman. The Cat pops a CD into his hat (really) and becomes Carmen Miranda with a bunch of fruit and

CONCEPT ART

TOP PHOTO
After the place has been totally trashed, it's time to play one last game, says the Cat. "It's called 'Clean up the House.'"

ABOVE
A computer illustration for the maze-like flume ride that climaxes the in-house chaos. The whole set was designed like a theme park ride, and then the technicians had to come in and figure out how to make it work.

bananas on his hat, and then a matador fighting a bull. He croons: "You can juggle work and play/But you have to know the way."

"The Cat's song was very challenging because within that number there are half a dozen hair, costume, makeup and lighting changes, along with visual effects and the song itself," sighs Welch. "It was just mind bogglingly difficult."

The juggling was a pretty neat move in its own right. "It's got some special effects, some in camera effects, some CGI, some cuts using doubles, CGI props—all the tricks are used in that one," says Welch.

"It took a long time but when I saw the first cut, I thought, 'It's great, it works.'"

Equally important to the mystique of the Cat—and just as complicated to film—

was the cleanup scene. This could turn out to be the most anticipated moment in the movie.

Everyone knows there's a mess coming. The question is, how's it going to be cleaned up?

With the cleanup machine, of course. "It does carpentry and plastering and electrical work and plumbing. It's insane. I'd love to have one," cracks Welch.

It may clean the house in thirty seconds but there was nothing easy about this machine. There were actually three of them, one for the Cat and two for the Things.

They were built in two months with the same process as the S.L.O.W., but they have radio-controlled electric wheelchairs inside. "Mike didn't operate it because he had too many things to do, and the Things were just nine-years-old,"

86

"There was a constant reassessment on a daily basis of how these things were going to fit together."

—Alex McDowell

ABOVE
Conrad prepares for his 'flight' down the stairs.

RIGHT
Splish splash, the Kids take a bath—or a car wash to be more exact. Yet another of the Cat's incredible inventions removes the purple slime from the Kids so their mother won't freak out.

says Tom Fisher, the man who built the machines.

With dozens of hands reaching out to do the work, the machines looked just like they were supposed to—like the ones in the book. "The cleanup machine is a good example of how we could transform the book into real form," says Welch. "We tried to get the character of Seuss' drawing and also exist in the real world."

The arms, most of them CG, come out from portals all around the machine with air blowers, jig saws and brushes. A few of the attachments were real and bounced around freely, or were manipulated by someone holding fishing line off camera.

"There were a lot of puppeteered hands and mechanical objects that we had to make work in a live action context," acknowledges McDowell.

At the same time, there was also the action of the cleanup machines tearing through the house. In one main shot they were pulled part of the way up the wall on tightly strung cables.

Another shot had one of the Things driving on the ceiling. This was simply filmed right side up and flipped in the processing. When the pieces were put together many months later, it was a combination of state-of-the art effects combined with old-fashioned in-camera tricks. Pretty basic filmmaking.

The most ambitious action scene in the film could actually be something out of a theme park. In the distorted house, overtaken by Seussian mayhem, Mrs. Kwan, the baby sitter, becomes a flume ride flowing on a river of purple ooze. The Cat and the kids hop on.

ABOVE
Welch created an actual indoor flume ride for the fun house scene. The final, enormously complicated scene was a combination of CGI and live action.

Luckily it wasn't the actress (Amy Hill), but a 12-foot-long fiberglass model moved along on a system of sophisticated conveyor belts. The main structure was like a roller coaster, 60-feet wide by 80-feet long and 35-feet high, made out of hard foam with a steel base constructed on stage 12 at Universal.

"We built the track for the ride and a large pit with a huge amount of running water and vapor rising," says McDowell.

Shooting the scene took on a little extra drama when Lubezki went right up to the last second before figuring out how to light tons of running water to give it a stunning purplish pink hue.

When you see the limousine Mrs. Kwan, as she was called on the set, plummeting down the really dynamic parts of the ride, most of that was done in the computer. But a surprising eighty percent of the footage of the actors on the ride was shot in camera, then smoothed out and enhanced with CGI.

"The challenge was finding shapes that fit with the rest of the movie," says Visual Effects Supervisor Doug Smith. "We wanted to combine the flow itself with the CG water and shots of the actors so it all looks real and doesn't fall apart." ⬇

Riding the Rapids in the Mother of all Messes

(top) The sleeping Mrs. Kwan doesn't look like an amusement park ride, but that's before the Things get loose and turn the house into "a launching pad for chaos." (middle) An early drawing of the Kids hanging ten on Mrs. Kwan as she cascades down the stairway. (above left) Jaremy Aiello paints the completed fiberglass dummy for the Baby Sitter Flume Ride. (above right) A mechanism was designed to make the dummy's head bang up and down as the kids rode her down the stairs.

CONCEPT ART

The Cat's Hat

What's a cat without a hat? "Without the hat I'm just your garden variety six-foot talking cat," says our hero. With the hat he can do almost anything. It's like a magic wand with stripes. Expanding on what the hat does in the book, the filmmakers invented about 15 new and wonderful kinds of hats.

Costume designer Rita Ryack, who was nominated for an Oscar for *Dr. Seuss' How the Grinch Stole Christmas*, started with a very, very tall hat. However, it looked too much like a Halloween costume. She made another out of silk taffeta that looked like a real formal top hat. It didn't work very well either. "We tried tall hats and fat hats. We tried corduroy, but it had no stretch. The hat had to do lots of tricks because really it's a character too," says Ryack.

ABOVE
Costume designer Rita Ryack checks out some eye-popping fabric (green, of course) with director Bo Welch on the lawn in Simi Valley. She was used to working with yellows and reds and had to adapt to the colors of the film. "As soon as I saw the original illustrations for the sets I was thrilled." she says.

In the book, the hat never looks exactly the same from one page to another, so the filmmakers were on their own creating the perfect brim, the ideal shape and the right color. One of the costume assistants got so tired of dyeing fabric red that she quit her job.

"It took forever," admits Welch, sighing. "I would get impatient and say, 'It's called *The Cat in the Hat*, where's the hat?'"

Finally, at the last minute, they came up with polar fleece, which gave the hat just the right texture and color.

"Hallelujah, that was our cat hat!" says Ryack.

But that was only the beginning of the hat tricks. "Bo would tell us what he wanted and then one of our prop designers would create something in the computer," explains Robin Miller. "Then we'd hand it over to someone who had to engineer this thing, make it work mechanically. They usually stomped and raved and screamed and said it's physically impossible, and ultimately we had it."

The hat is full of bizarre Seussian contraptions. It morphs into a chef's hat and the Cat is a cook; a periscope pops out of the top and he looks over a hedge for a lost dog; a CD player opens up and he does a musical number. The hat is stacked with bananas and fruit á la Carmen Miranda, and inflates like an airbag when he crashes his car. A mirror springs out of another hat and turns the Cat into a doctor.

The specialty hats were all mechanically complex. As many as three

Rita's sketchbook

LITTLE GIRLS
LIKE NAIL
POLISH

RAN OUT
O'SPACE
FOR

MATCHING
PUMPS

HEY!
CALVIN IS AN ANAGRAM
OF ANVIL (with a C)
So... he could wear
CANVIL KLEIN
Jockeys!!
CANVILKLEIN-GET IT?

RITA'S CREATIONS COME TO LIFE

Conrad represented the chaotic personality so Ryack
dressed him in hot colors. He wears his pants low like a
home boy and his thick, sloppy sneakers with yellow
stripes are actually taken from a Seuss drawing. Sally's
costumes, like her little sweater and starched jumper,
are designed to make her look prim and uptight. Her
look is loosely adapted from the book. The mom, who
we never see in the book, gets to wear the only pink in
the movie because she's the yuppie mommy. Among
the many hats Ryack designed for the Cat, was the
Carmen Miranda hat topped with fruit. It looked so
good, you could eat it.

Rita Ryack's Films as Costume Designer

*Academy Award® nomination

Lots of hats for Cats

puppeteers would manipulate a hat from off camera, while engineers handled remote controls.

The costume department wound up making sixteen hats in triplicates. And not just the ones for Mike Myers; his double and stunt cats all had to have hats. Sometimes it seemed as if Bartholomew Cubbins had arrived with his 500 hats! "There were a lot of hats walking around on the set," agrees Ryack. "It was a little disorienting at times."

Just keeping the hat on Myers' head was an engineering feat in itself. The cat's ears prevented the hat from fitting snugly on his head, so after much experimentation the solution was to hold the hat on with a ring of magnets attached to Myers' head with a skull cap. This worked just fine, and even in stunt scenes when the cat turned upside down, the hat stayed put.

Steve Johnson, special make-up effects supervisor who developed the idea for the magnets, did have one worry. "I was afraid someone would say Mike's not funny anymore. There was a lot of magnetic resonance going on around his brain," he laughs. 🎙

> The cat's hat is the most recognizable hat in the world, except for maybe the Pope's.

RITA RYACK costume designer

Baby, You Can Drive My Car

CONCEPT ART

CONCEPT ART

THE FLYING
S.L.O.W.

CAT IN THE HAT ART DEPARTMENT   07-09-02
FINISHED COMPUTER MODEL OF THE SLOW

ABOVE
Welch wanted to capture the wit of the Seussian world, seen here in a conceptual drawing. "The joke is that everyone drives a lovely little electric hybrid car of the same color, except the Cat," says Welch. "There's something chaotic about his car."

Observant readers might notice that there is no car in *Dr. Seuss's "The Cat in the Hat."* However, in the movie the kids use it to chase after their runaway dog. The pet is really just a convenient way to move the story outside the house.

When Quinn captures the dog and drives off in his T-Bird, the Cat suggests they follow in his car. "You have a car?" Conrad is amazed. The Cat opens the garage and there it is—a super cool H2 Hummer. The kids are impressed. "Wow, this is so cool," says Conrad. But that's just the dust cover. The Cat rips it off and underneath is, well, a jalopy that looks like something the junkyard just coughed up.

"At the same time it's cool in its own way," says Welch. "I wanted something that would make you smile. And it's cool within the personality and sensibility of the Cat, who is slightly crazy, anarchic. The Cat's solutions to things aren't always the most practical, but they're fun."

The first thing you notice about the car is that it's only got three wheels. The Cat calls it his Super Luxurious Omnidirectional Whatchamajigger, or S.L.O.W. for short. It started with a sketch by Welch inspired by a mad inventor named Heath Robinson.

It's part-car, part-boat, with wood side paneling, a red and white striped pointy nose and wings that make you think it could fly (at one point it was going to have helicopter propellers).

The actual look was created by car designer Harold Belker. "He was going from designing the high tech Lexus for 'Minority Report' to this. So we had to lock him in a padded cell and beat him up for a few days," jokes Alex McDowell.

Once the shock wore off, Belker came up with the concept that was converted into three-dimensional drawings in the computer and tweaked some more. When the dimensions were absolutely

CONCEPT ART

GET READY SWITCHES

PUMP UP/DOWN TO START HELICOPTER

TURN SIGNAL
WITH DIRECT
RESPONSE LEVER

WINDOW CRANK

COLOR OF EXHAUST SWITCH

SPEED OF FRONT NOSE

OIL PRESSURE METER

SUPER FAN

SPEEDOMETER

GLOVE COMP.

"CHICKEN" BUTTON

HOLD ON BAR

LIGHT SWITCH

OLD STYLE RADIO

20 GEAR SHIFTER

SUPER ARTICULATING
CUP-HOLDER

STEERING WHEEL

080202

HAROLD BELKER

CAT IN THE HAT ART DEPARTMENT
SLOW DASH-BOARD LAYOUT

ABOVE

The interior of the S.L.O.W. was part
Seuss and part Salvador Dali. Belker
managed to make it look old fashioned
and futuristic at the same time

BELOW

Car designer Harold Belker fashioned
the S.L.O.W. after a sketch by Welch,
who wanted a half-car, half-boat look
with wood side panels and wings that
could almost fly.

CONCEPT ART

HARALD BELKER

ABOVE
Welch chats with Breslin
to see if he's got his
seat belt on.

NEXT PAGE
It's amazing how a small
element, like a seussian
sky, can make or break
a shot. (above) Shot of
the S.L.O.W without the
extra CGI sky and color
correction. (below) A
test shot with the CGI
sky and background
elements in place.

accurate, a foam model was built.

The model and blueprints were then shipped off to special effects coordinator Tom Fisher, who worked out the engineering for the car. Meanwhile, the sculptors were casting the body parts in fiberglass and painting them metallic silver. Fisher and his team of twelve put the pieces together from the bottom up in four months.

"It's designed to look as if a bad inventor was trying to make a car that would go fast but really didn't work very well," says McDowell, "and everything kind of bumps and explodes and smoke pours out of it and flames come out of the back."

With its two wheels in front and one wheel in back, the car handles like a wheelbarrow or a tricycle facing backwards. Each wheel turns separately so the car wobbles from side to side, moves sideways like a crab or spins around in circles. Because the Cat gives the steering wheel to the kids and then all three of them drive (even the fish gets a steering wheel), there was no way the actors could really be handling the car.

The real driver is sitting out of sight behind the back seat watching three monitors and operating all the controls. This is known as a blind driver in the business. If you think it's easy, you try it sometime.

It took the driver three months to learn how to do it. Once he mastered the driving, the car could cruise along at 45 mph and turn on a dime.

The S.L.O.W. is really a perfect Seussian contraption. If the Cat in the book had a car, it would be clunky, impractical and ingenuous just like this one.

"It's the neatest thing," says Dakota Fanning, who at the age of nine got to drive for the first time. "It has red smoke coming out the back that looks like fire. It's so neat."

Wild Things

Who are the Things? Are they real, are they fantasy? Are they male or female? "That was the question I kept getting from everyone, including the studio, about Thing One and Thing Two," says Welch. "They wanted to know, are they human, puppets, CG?" Welch decided to cast nine and eleven-year old girls — dancers and gymnasts — as the creatures who escape the Cat's crate.

"My experience is that whenever you can get real people in front of the camera it's preferable." "So they were little girls in prosthetic makeup," he continues. "But that doesn't mean the Things were girls. We're not saying," he says coyly.

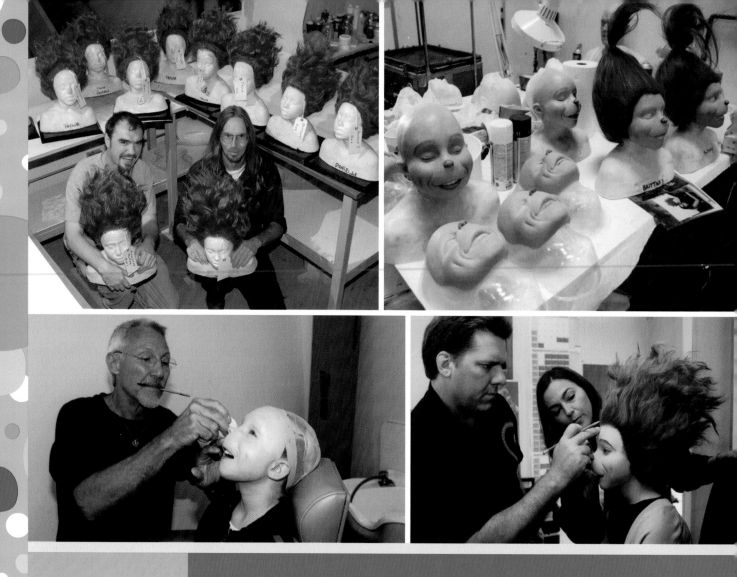

ABOVE
(clockwise from upper left)
John Shea and Jim Beinke
pose with the many wigs
they created for Thing 1 &
Thing 2. The idea was to
make them bounce and act
crazy, just like the Things;
Rubber masks for the Things
in various stages of
completion; James Rohland
and Margie Latinopoulos
apply the final touches to
the Thing make-up and wig;
Lance Anderson applies the
full face cover and muzzle
around the mouth.

Casting was quite an adventure in itself. Hundreds of kids showed up, a few even wearing blue wigs they had made.

"It was bizarre,' says Welch. "We auditioned gymnasts and dancers for days and days, hearing the same audition music over and over again, and watching these amazingly talented kids come out and flip around and dance."

The downside was that kids this age could only work a certain number of hours a day, and out of that, makeup took three hours. So Welch cast four girls as the Things to give himself more time and flexibility.

"That worked out great. After a while there were subtle differences in what they could do and I could tell them apart," he says.

In terms of makeup, the idea was to give the Things as much expression as possible. So while a very soft customized rubber mask covered the girls' faces, it was thin enough around the eyes and the movement areas to allow their personality to come through.

Another trick Steve Johnson and his makeup team did was to make really big dentures for the girls that stretched out their mouths about an inch. When the mold for the mask was taken, the mouth was already puffed out and distorted. This was a way of controlling their facial expression from the inside out, and creating kind of a muzzle around the mouth that was faithful to the book.

"These Things will not bite you, they want to have fun.
So without further ado, meet Thing Two and Thing One."
— THE CAT

And to top it off, Johnson created a wild blue wig. "We really wanted to get them to bounce and be insane," he says.

The wigs were built on vacuum-formed skull caps that had springs and wires all over them, covered by sheaths of custom fur fabric. The blue hair was synthetic and it did bounce and shake like crazy.

"I would have to say that the Things are the most effective makeup to come out of my studio, because when people see them they just don't know what to think," says Johnson, proudly.

Welch admits that the Things walk a fine line between grotesque and amusing. "When they were done wrong, they were creepy; when they were right they were adorable, but still slightly off-putting. Although they speak gibberish, we didn't want them to be like creepy aliens running around the house."

Using real girls instead of CGI gave Welch the feeling that the Things were like out-of-control kids, taken to the max. His hope was to have the girls do as much as humanly possible and then enhance that with CG, so people will be left wondering, "How did they do that?"

"Otherwise it's just a stage show," says Welch.

It also helped that the girls were into performing so much. "They enjoyed the makeup and the attention and that really made a difference," says Johnson. "When they put on the makeup they became these characters. They were really fun and really cute."

Sean Hayes, who wasn't around on the set and didn't see the Things until he started to record the voice of the fish, couldn't believe his eyes. "I was like, 'Wow!' They blew me away. They were the closest thing I saw to the book."

ABOVE
Thanks to Spencer, the Things are wild in the streets of Anville.

107

The Things as played by (from left to right) Danielle Chuchrun, Brittany Oaks, Talia Prairie and Taylor Rice

"They enjoyed the makeup and the attention and that really made a difference. When they put on the makeup they became these characters. They were really fun and really cute."

— **Steve Johnson**
about the actors who played
Thing 1 and Thing 2

THE CAT'S TOYS

There are lots of things in *Dr. Seuss' The Cat in the Hat* movie that aren't in the book—but they could have been. For instance, there's an amazing foot-and-a-half mechanical chicken that pops out of the hood of the S.L.O.W. If a traffic light is red and you don't want to stop, the chicken sprays the light with green paint. (Never mind that this causes an accident.)

"We thought what would Dr. Seuss do if he had to spray green paint on something? And we came up with the chicken," chirps Alex McDowell.

There is a kind of goofball logic at work here. Things do happen for a reason, just not the obvious one. This is never more apparent than in the stunning collection of props and contraptions designed for the film.

CONCEPT ART

"These are some of the most spectacular props in film history; they're unbelievable," adds McDowell.

It's no doubt that prop master Robin Miller was a busy man on this production. He estimates that his department made

THIS PAGE
Concept art of the Cat holding Phunometer and, on the right page, the final full-scale movie prop.

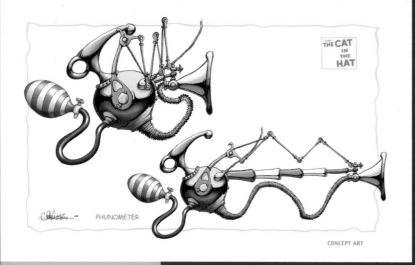

PHUNOMETER

THE CAT IN THE HAT

CONCEPT ART

the prop would get tweaked and evolve into its final form. "For this one particular prop, the Phunometer, I think there were 43 different versions designed," says Miller. "Beautiful renderings, I mean frameable computer drawings of this thing."

The Phunometer is a device the Cat uses to measure the balance between chaos and order in the kids. It looks like a crazy stethoscope with a gauge that registers their chaos level. The Phunometer says Sally is a "Control Freak," and it emits a low-pitched hum. For Conrad the dial shoots to the other side and says "Rule Breaker," and the machine gives off a high-pitched squeal.

This is one of the pivotal scenes in the movie because it sets up the whole notion of balancing chaos and order. "The Phunometer grew out of needing a physical object that would explain that theory," says Welch. "The Phunometer was created to have some physical way of demonstrating an otherwise abstract principle."

THIS PAGE
(above) Another of the designs for the Phunometer;

(below) The crab is actually the lock that keeps the Things in the crate.

115 items used by the Cat, what they call hero props.

"The production designer decides what the look of the movie is and we read the script and figure out what props are needed and how they interact with the actors. Then we design them accordingly and finally build them."

Miller, who handled props for *The Adams Family,* says that film was a good primer for *The Cat in the Hat.* "We had to do things that were surreal. None of that stuff existed in our world so it had to be created from the ground up."

For *The Cat in the Hat,* designers would do sketches on a computer and eventually

CONCEPT ART

MADE IN THE PHILIPPINES

ABOVE
While Conrad makes a mess, Sally has her nose buried in her PDA making her to do list, which includes items like: "Creating lasting childhood memories," "Be spontaneous" and "Amend will."

RIGHT
The 'lock' does a little exploring of its own.

ABOVE
A computer illustration for the Cat's Kupkake-inator (inset) vs. the real prop. It's a typical clunky device that doesn't really do what it's supposed to, but the Cat thinks it does.

The Cat's props had an intentionally low tech feel to them. In the modern world, the Phunometer would have been a hand-held digital device. Instead, it's a silly, cumbersome contraption in keeping with the spirit of the book. Still, it took three people to operate.

Another clunky device was the Kupkake-inator. Originally the idea for this scene was much simpler—putting a baking tray in the oven and watching it explode. But close to shooting, Myers had an inspiration, as he often did. His idea was to do it as a parody of an infomercial. So the machine had to be redesigned in a hurry and wound up as a cross between a pressure cooker and an oven.

"The joke is everyone has a breadmaker or something in their kitchen that's more

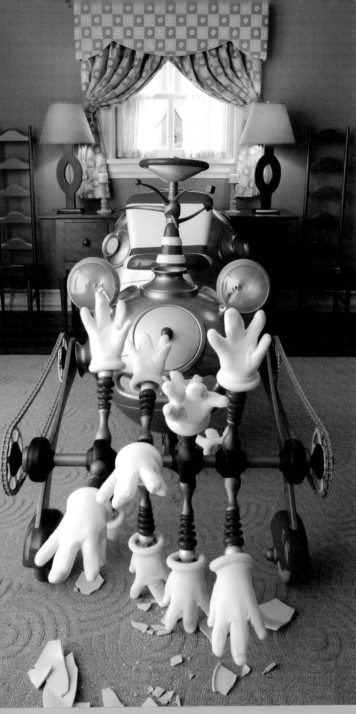

THE CAT IN THE HAT

complicated than it needs to be," says Welch. "It's very Williams Sonoma forties-looking, but it's heavy and messy and noisy, definitely a contraption from the aesthetic of the Cat. Then when it explodes, he acts as if that's what it does. 'Oh, yes, they're done.'"

But easier said than done. The Kupkake-inator took months to design and was changing right up until—and during—shooting. One operator hid under the table as the cake batter was stuffed into the machine while another guy operated it with remote controls.

Ultimately, Myers had to be comfortable with the gadgets. "It's not like anyone knew how these items worked," says Miller. "Mike was the sole guy standing up there with the silly thing in his hand and somehow had to make it all funny."

ABOVE
The Cat and Thing clean-up machines next to their prototype designs.

A River Runs Through IT

Before starting to design the computer animation for the fish character, animation supervisor Craig Talmy asked director Bo Welch what was his inspiration for the personality of the fish. Welch said to think of it as Barney Fife, the neurotic worrywart from the old Andy Griffith Show.

So Talmy sat down and watched Barney Fife for weeks, looking for moments he could apply to the fish's performance.

But getting the personality of the animated fish may have been the easy part. Rhythm & Hues, the company developing the computer-generated imagery (CGI), had created a higher number of shots for other films, but for sheer diversity, *The Cat* was a monster.

Welch had hoped to use less CGI and more real elements (known as "practical" shots in the business). "Tonally, flashy computer-generated imagery doesn't seem to be appropriate for Dr. Seuss," he says.

"There's a joy and a lightness and a silliness you get with real objects as opposed to CG. But, I haven't met a good talking fish yet, so, naturally the fish is CG."

The driving force for the fish was Seuss' image in the book. After initial sketches, a rubber model was made from 3D computer drawings. This was then used as a prop on the set during shooting while a stand-in recited the fish's lines.

Back in the lab was where the real fishing was going on. "The fish was probably the most complicated character to design because we were trying to find a place between reality and fantasy," says McDowell.

The first technical problem to solve: How do you make the scales and fins look real with life-like transparency and iridescence?

If you've looked at a fish up close lately, you know it can be a pretty slimy thing. The filmmakers wanted to capture that look, as well as different degrees of wetness at different times.

ABOVE
Final concept render of the fish

LEFT
One of the challenges for Rhythm & Hues in creating the CGI fish was making the eyes look real. The iris is like a human eye and the white is like a fish eye. Light refracts off the eyes and they change shape. just like human eyes.

This called for Rhythm & Hues to break new technical ground with a process called "global illumination." It required taking a 360 degree photograph of the set and surrounding the fish with this information inside the computer, then mapping the reflections and lighting from the real shot back onto the fish. Pretty sophisticated stuff.

The work was so exacting that if you look closely at the cornea of the fish's eye, you'll see light from the background being refracted. "We worked very hard on this," says Doug Smith, Rhythm & Hues visual effects supervisor. "When you see the fish's eyes turn, you'll see the shape change and light bouncing off it like human eyes."

To make matters even more complex, the fish also needed to move through water in a bowl and a jar. The amount of detail was mind boggling. "Some of the key people were saying it's just a simple fish, but it was incredibly complex," says Smith. "The rendering time was gigantic."

Once all the information was entered into the computer, it took dozens of hours for the computer to do its calculations and finish a single frame of film. One scene could be hundreds of frames. No wonder it took nearly eight months from design to first finished shot.

CONCEPT ART

While Rhythm & Hues was off fishing, it was also working on another problem almost as gnarly—the house that goes haywire after the Things get loose. This is not just about a broken lamp or a vase that needs to be glued, there's a river of purple slime running through it.

"This was the single most difficult set," says McDowell. "It was pure 3D set design using architectural software to create the physical space. You couldn't do this any other way, you couldn't draw this with a pencil, it was too wild and there were too many dimensions."

CONCEPT ART

Just like in the book, the Things escape from a red crate, but here it's a portal to a Seussian world of chaos. A tornado explodes out of the box, along with a purple jelly-like substance that floats through the house.

"Bo coined the term 'chicken fat' for the ooze because it had that consistency," says Smith. "It comes out of the box and is sucked up by the tornado. Giant chunks of chicken fat are flying around the room, tendrils of it are coming out of the box."

Meanwhile, the tornado is spinning out of control and the kids are sucked in and out of the vortex. At one point, even Alec Baldwin's head is seen spinning in the mess. "That was a relatively late wrinkle to the story line," says Smith. "Incorporating his face is supposed to make the situation more threatening." 🎤

ABOVE
On this show even the fish had a stand-in. The animated fish was added to the scene later. Meanwhile, a rubber model of the fish in Conrad's backpack is ready for his close-up, Mr. De Mille.

BOTTOM LEFT
A top down view of the twisted house and Kwan ride.

121

Animal Kingdoms

What would happen if the Cat and the Things came to your house? No, they're not coming to make a mess. In a variety of toys, video games and play things, *Dr. Seuss' The Cat in the Hat* is bringing its sense of fun and imagination to your home.

The inventive folks at Vivendi Universal Games have been inspired by the unique visual style of movie and have created the

BELOW
Creatures strange and wondrous confront our hero thoughout his adventure. You'd best stay alert.

official video game for PC, PlayStation 2, Xbox and Game Boy Advance. The Cat, the Things and some new surprises along the way bring the movie magic home for kids, who may have a hard time getting mom and dad away from the screen.

The game offers fans an interactive extension of the film experience, explains producer Stephen Townsend. "We're inviting gamers to play as the Cat and delve more deeply into the fanciful world that fans were introduced to over 45 years ago."

That's putting it mildly. Throughout more than 20 levels presented in stunning 3D, the game allows you to follow the film's storyline complete with familiar characters, hilarious one-liners and one frustrated fish, who occasionally offers hints when not taking playful shots at the hero.

The Seussian whimsy and imaginative design created by Welch and McDowell comes to life in brightly colored levels concealed in grandfather clocks,

SCREEN SHOT

SCREEN SHOT

SCREEN SHOT

SCREEN SHOT

SCREEN SHOT

potted plants, record players and other exotic locales.

After Conrad picks the crab lock that keeps the Things safely in their crate, and his pet dog, Nevins, runs off with the lock, all kinds of chaos erupts in the house. It's the player's job to recover the three pieces of the crab lock and get the house back to normal before mom comes home.

Based on the movie and set in the same house, the program features one whole level inspired by a sequence from the film. In addition, there are some new and fun elements not in the movie.

"We've created over 15 original creatures especially for the adventure, such as the Dino-sore, the Grab Crab and Greeny Meany," says Townsend. "Other goodies include lots of bonus areas, a secret level and other surprises I'd rather not spoil by mentioning."

Play is suitably fast-paced and involves typical tasks such as capturing creatures with bubbles, floating over pits with an umbrella and collecting keys that unlock challenging bonus stages. Multiple endings, picture galleries featuring images from the film are also included.

Just like the movie, it's a first-class production. 'It's a beautiful game to look at and good clean fun for the whole family," adds Townsend. "Parents can play it freely with their kids and have just as much fun. The title truly reflects the humor indicative of the film."

In a way the video game compliments the incredible artistry of the film. "Without the movie, we never would have been able to come up with all this stuff," says Townsend. "The film is the starting point for everything. We just tried to take it to another level." 🎤 — *Scott Steinberg*

ABOVE
It's raining, it's pouring, the old cat is soaring... thanks to his trusty umbrella.

INSET
Topsy-turvy worlds of whimsy lurk inside the most mundane of household objects, where the adventure is set.

Animal Kingdoms

CAT TREATS

We all know *Dr. Seuss' The Cat in the Hat* is the cat's meow, but why should the fun stop there?

Inspired by the film's imaginative style, manufacturers are producing wondrous diversions of all shapes and sizes for Cat fanciers everywhere.

From bathroom accessories to bedding and stylish baseball caps, both adults and children alike will find numerous surprises in store. Here's a look at some of the more inventive items that are sure to catch your eye.

— *Scott Steinberg*

Cat Got Your Fun?

From: Play Along
Mike Myers has been immortalized as the famed feline, complete with signature hat and umbrella. Even the pesky fish who troubles him throughout the movie is represented here. Amusingly, the piscine pest actually recites lines from the film to boot.
www.playalong.com

Cat in the Hat Skateboard

From: Franklin Sports
Bedecked with the Cat's image on its bottom and an outline of his body on its top, this skateboard's sure to make a statement. Mount its 28" surface and you'll be in for the ride of your life. Gnarly, man.
www.franklinsports.com

Shoes & Slippers

From: Brown Shoe

Boys and girls can bolster their wardrobe with boots and shoes featuring the likenesses of the Cat, Thing 1 and Thing 2. All footwear is offered in children's sizes 5-3. Awesome fuzzy slipper models are also in production for both kids and adults.

www.brownshoe.com

Zip-Zap Starter Kit

From: Radio Shack

Why watch the Things trash the house when they could be racing through it? Armed with the included 49Mhz radio-controller and a slick mini-car model that includes optional figurines, you can turn any table into a speedway.

www.radioshack.com

Fish Light

From: Radio Shack

Brighten the darkest night with a little help from everyone's favorite talking goldfish. A sturdy plastic casing and mouth-mounted bulb render it night indestructible. You wouldn't believe how handy the device comes in for finding Thing 1 and Thing 2.

www.radioshack.com

Interactive Talking Plush

From: Play Along

At 18" in size with proportional parts, no child could resist tugging the Cat's tail. Luckily, doing so triggers pre-recorded speech clips, as does squeezing the doll's hands and feet. Storybook functions let the plush read along with little ones.

www.playalong.com

Super-Luxurious Omni-directional Whatchamajigger

From: Play Along

The Cat prefers riding in style. Now you can too with his patented Super-Luxurious Omni-directional Whatchamajigger (S.L.O.W) vehicle. Pop-up spray cannon, spinning turbo cone and jet afterburner add class to an already outlandish concept car. Radio-control model also available from Radio Shack.

www.playalong.com

Happy Endings

The Cat in the Hat was timely when Theodor Geisel wrote it in 1957. Perhaps it is even more so today.

"The world of *The Cat In The Hat* is more like the world we are living in now," says Grazer. "And the story lends itself to modern themes."

It's a timeless tale. A mother goes out and leaves her children on their own to discover...whatever. Anything is possible if they know where to look. Unfortunately, they don't—but the Cat does.

"The cat is a teacher, a philosopher who's giving this family a lesson in chaos theory," says Welch. "It's like a line from the book: 'It's fun to have fun but you have to know how.' That's what the movie is about, how to have fun."

The thing that keeps the kids from having fun then—and now—is a loss of imagination. *The Cat In the Hat* is there to say, 'you have all of the power within you, you have it, you just have to appreciate it,'" says Grazer. "It's very mythological."

The simple tools for fun that Seuss was writing about in the fifties have become even harder to find today. Grazer says when he was getting ready to make *Dr. Seuss' The Cat in the Hat, Time* and *Newsweek* were coincidentally running stories about how technology has taken something away from kids.

And hopefully, this movie gives some of it back. Just as the Cat inspires a sense of joy using everyday play things, the filmmakers tried to keep things simple. "Bo has been keeping this pure, childlike view of why we're making this movie and who it's for," says McDowell. "It's very un-cynical and un-adult."

The doors are too big, the windows are too large, the house is oversized—just as a child would see it. The film is designed to appeal to the whimsy in children—and in all of us.

"Somehow, *The Cat*, or *The Grinch* reach you on a primordial level. That's why they have such staying power," says Grazer. "When people think of *The Cat in the Hat* my hope is that they will think of the movie, just as they do with *The Grinch*. My hope is that it will have the same resonance," says Grazer.

"It's going to be a really delightful film," predicts McDowell, "and I think a film that harkens back to the *Wizard of Oz* or *Willy Wonka & the Chocolate Factory* more than contemporary kids' movies."

For many of the cast and crew it was the most fun they ever had making a movie, and were sad to leave the Seussian world.

"I hope that people see the humor in what we've done," says McDowell. "I hope people get transported by the world we've built. I think there's a real magic to what's been created."

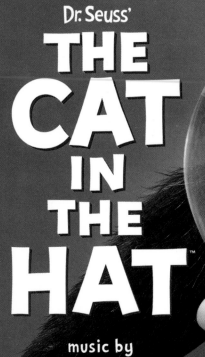

original motion picture soundtrack

Dr. Seuss'
THE
CAT
IN
THE
HAT™

music by
David Newman

CATS WITH HATS ONLY!

SPECIAL MINI-POSTER INSIDE!

DECCA RECORDS — A UNIVERSAL MUSIC COMPANY · UMG SOUNDTRACKS · UNIVERSAL · DREAMWORKS PICTURES · IMAGINE

www.universalclassics.com